A
MOTHER'S
CIRCLE

Wisdom and Reassurance from Other Mothers on Your First Year with Baby

**JEAN KUNHARDT, M.A.,
LISA SPIEGEL, M.A., AND
SANDRA K. BASILE**

AVON BOOKS  NEW YORK

A MOTHER'S CIRCLE is an original publication of Avon Books. This work has never before appeared in book form.

AVON BOOKS
A division of
The Hearst Corporation
1350 Avenue of the Americas
New York, New York 10019

Copyright © 1996 by Jean Kunhardt, Lisa Spiegel, and Sandra Kunhardt Basile
Cover illustration by Synthia Saint James
Published by arrangement with the authors
Library of Congress Catalog Card Number: 95-40983
ISBN: 0-380-77802-5

Library of Congress Cataloging in Publication Data:
Kunhardt, Jean.
    A mother's circle: wisdom and reassurance from other mothers on your first year with baby / Jean Kunhardt, Lisa Spiegel, and Sandra K. Basile.
        p. cm.
1. Mothers—New York (N.Y.)—Case studies. 2. Motherhood—New York (N.Y.)—Case studies. 3. Mother and infant—New York (N.Y.)—Case studies. I. Spiegel, Lisa. II. Basile, Sandra K. III. Title.
HQ759.K85   1996   95-40983
306.874'3'097471—dc20   CIP

First Avon Books Trade Printing: March 1996

AVON TRADEMARK REG. U.S. PAT. OFF. AND IN OTHER COUNTRIES, MARCA REGISTRADA, HECHO EN U.S.A.

Printed in the U.S.A.

OPM   10 9 8 7 6 5 4 3 2 1

To our mothers, with love
J.K.   L.S.   S.K.B.

∾ ACKNOWLEDGMENTS ∾

We would like to thank our families for their sustaining confidence, inspiration, and generous humor throughout the writing of this book. To Fred. To Irwin. To Frank. To Eliza and Suzannah. To Audrey and Maris. To Giulia and Anna. To the Kunhardt family. To the Spiegel family.

Dr. Marie Keith and Dr. Robert Coffey of the Soho Pediatric Group shared a vision with us and have provided ongoing support in its realization. We thank them both. Great love to Evelyn Dickey, M.A., for getting us together.

For their mentorship and guidance we are grateful to Dr. Anni Bergman, Dr. Barbara Blum, and Bonnie Beck, C.S.W. Thank you to Barbara Melson, M.S., ADTR, for her commitment to the Soho Parenting Center and her sensitive work with families there.

We are indebted to all of the families who have participated in ParenTalk and the Soho Parenting Center. This book in many ways is their story. By allowing us a window into the intimacy and power of parent-child relationships they have stretched our capacities for compassion and have helped us to better understand ourselves. We would also like to express our appreciation to all those who were interviewed at length for this book. We hope we have done justice to their thoughts and feelings.

Thank you to Miriam Altshuler, our agent. Her dedication to this book, in all of its forms, her insight, encouragement, and efforts on our behalf have been exceptional. And we thank Gwen Montgomery, our editor, for her confidence, patience, and sensitive editing. It was always an asset and a blessing to work with professionals who were themselves new mothers. For her skillful copy editing, thanks also go to Sara Schwager.

A personal note of thanks from Sandra Kunhardt Basile goes to Susan King and Lisa Basile for their careful reading of the manuscript and for their suggestions along the way. For her early interest and encouragement, thank you to Lynda Grimm. For her sage advice thank you to Hester Kaplan. For his medical wisdom and his gift of time, I am grateful to Dr. Wilson Utter of Waterman Pediatrics. For teaching me about what makes a story come alive, thank you to Peter W. Kunhardt. For their tender care of my very young children, thanks go also to Mary Ryan, Bonnie Yoder, Shannon Guilderson, and Esther Hayes. *Mille grazie* to Francis and Gloria Basile for their loving and generous encouragement. And to the two people whose belief in my writing and invaluable help were critical to the completion of this project, thank you beyond words to my husband and my father.

Finally, the three of us would like to thank one another for being each other's best friends, sisters, colleagues, mentors, lifelines. This book has been a journey for each of us, with ups and downs, but ever-present faith and mutual love.

J.K., L.S., S.K.B.

Contents

A
MOTHER'S
CIRCLE

Foreword

The renowned child psychoanalyst D.W. Winnicott is often quoted as having said that there is no such thing as a baby: there is only a baby with a mother. Lisa Spiegel and Jean Kunhardt's work with mothers and babies grows out of the realization of the importance of the mother-baby dyad and the need to support the development of both.

In 1959, under the leadership of Margaret S. Mahler, I was part of a group of psychoanalytic researchers who began an intensive, observational study of mother-child pairs in an indoor playground-like setting in New York City (Mahler, Pine and Bergman 1975). Mothers came with their infants and toddlers and spent the mornings talking with each other while their children played. Participant-observers moved about freely, interacting with both mothers and children. There was concern at the outset about how we would find mothers willing to take part in a study that required them to come with their babies four times a week to be observed, especially since we made it clear we were not going to give them advice about child care. To everyone's surprise, throughout the eight years of the observational study, recruitment of mother-child pairs never was a problem. At first we recruited mothers through a nursery school that was in the same building as the research center, but before long they came on their own, having heard about us by word of mouth.

What appeared to attract these mothers was the friendly, cheerful environment where their children could play safely and where participant-observers were available to both children and mothers in a supportive and interested way. Over time, we began to understand how isolated mothers can be, especially when little community or extended family support is available. New mothers often feel very much alone at this time of critical importance to their own and their family's well-being. They often feel excluded from the world of adults. They experience a loss of their former selves. Our study, then, filled an otherwise unspoken and sometimes unrecognized need among these new mothers for a community of supportive adults.

An important aspect of the design of our project was the continuity of our availability. Because of this continuity, we not only became part of the mothers' and children's worlds during the years we were with them, but we also became part of their internal worlds, remembered not for what we did or said, but for our presence and continued interest. More than twenty years later, mothers and their now-adult children continue to participate in follow-up interviews. Even though the adult-children don't remember much of the actual study or the people involved with them, they nevertheless derive satisfaction from the knowledge that they had been observed and known when they were young children. Thus, these families are willing and often eager to resume a connection that was first made during the period uniquely transforming to both mothers and infants.

Winnicott (1956) describes the state of the new mother, "primary maternal preoccupation," as a temporary stage necessary for the mother in the care of her newborn. More recently, Daniel Stern (1995), who is well-known for his studies of the world of the infant, has formulated his thoughts about motherhood, which he portrays as a unique psychic organization with conflicts and fears distinct from any others. Stern feels that a new mother's psychic energy is uniquely dedicated to the task of helping the new baby to survive. He speaks to the new mother's need to be supported in this task by her own mother and describes how new mothers seek the support and company of other women.

In our society there is generally not very much support given to mothers during the delicate and challenging transition to motherhood. A new mother often faces extremely difficult choices about how to balance the need to continue her former life, including her career, with her new role as a mother. Mothers may find themselves isolated and alone *with* their new baby, or they may find themselves isolated *from* their new baby whose care then has to be largely taken on by other caretakers. How each mother resolves these particular dilemmas will depend on the nature and demands of her career, her financial resources, the support her spouse and other family members are able to offer, and on how she resolves the internal conflict between her wish to maintain her former life and interests and her wish to relinquish everything else in favor of her new role as a mother. No matter what the choice, something has to be given up, and some loss has to be accepted.

While it is true that mothers come to motherhood with an already-established identity, it is equally true that motherhood provides new opportunities to widen and deepen and even to alter the sense of who one is in the world. Our original research project on the separation-individuation process (Mahler, Pine and Bergman 1975) underemphasized the new mother's process because at the time the thinking was that the process was completed—that the mothers had already achieved a fully consolidated sense of identity. Since then, infant development researchers (Stern, 1975; Brazelton and Cramer, 1990) have more fully explored the interactive nature of the mother-infant relationship and have coined new concepts, such as "mutual regulation" and "attunement." We are now at the point where aspects of separation-individuation theory can be rethought in terms of the phases of the mother's development and her need to establish a new self as a mother. Can we speak of the psychological birth of the mother as we are now used to speaking of the psychological birth of the infant?

A Mother's Circle has emerged from the work of two dedicated specialists who recognize the interwoven developmental experiences of mothers and babies. Its eight chapters alternate between those topics which preoccupy mothers about their new babies' development and those that deal with the changes that take place in mothers themselves as they become immersed in this new and unique phase in their lives. I know of no other book that balances discussions of baby-tending such as "The Importance of Sleep," "The Fear of Spoiling," and "Feeding and Nurturing," with issues concerning a mother's life that are more separate from her baby, such as "Work and Motherhood," "Changes in Your Marriage," and "Changes in Your Body."

The book's closing chapter, "Attachment and Separation," deals with the very issues I have been emphasizing. How much separation will interfere with the process of attachment for both mother and baby? How much attachment could interfere with becoming separate, as experienced for the first time by the baby and re-experienced by the mother? These questions are also given recognition in the chapter entitled, "The Legacy of Your Own Mother," in which the new mother is taken back to the roots of her identity as she begins to define herself anew by her experience of being a mother.

While *A Mother's Circle* focuses on mothers and babies, interviews with fathers are included in the chapters entitled, "Changes in Your Marriage," and "The Importance of Sleep." Men describe their reponses to fatherhood, their feelings about their baby's impact on their marriage, and the changes they see in their spouses. While in recent years much work has been done on the father-infant relationship, this book contributes to our understanding of the baby's impact on the father himself and on the intimacy of the marital relationship.

The needs of new mothers have been met in an important and special way by Lisa Spiegel and Jean Kunhardt, who have been conducting mother-baby groups for nearly ten years. In a safe and supporting environment, they have encouraged new mothers to speak freely about their fears and concerns. As leaders and interpreters for these groups, they have allowed the internal experience of new mothers to become one that is put into words, clarified, and shared.

A Mother's Circle is based on Kunhardt and Spiegel's insights gained from working with groups of mothers as they talk together about the new issues in their lives that derive from their newly born identities as mothers. Listening and speaking to mothers in groups is a different experience from conducting individual consultation, different in part because of the fullness of what is communicated, but different also because of the subtle enactments that take place in groups. *A Mother's Circle* communicates some of that experience to new mothers who often have to struggle with these important issues on their own.

I hope that reading about what other mothers and fathers say and think will stimulate mothers who read this book to seek out places where they, too, can share some of their concerns and fears about motherhood that would otherwise remain unspoken. *A Mother's Circle* will help mothers as they go through the exhilarating and joyful, but sometimes frightening and lonely process of transformation to motherhood, to begin to break the isolation, and engage in the dialogue.

Dr. Anni Bergman

Bergman, A. (1985) The mother's experience during the earliest phases of infant development. In Anthony & Pollock (Eds.) *Parental Influences in Health and Disease*. Boston: Little Brown & Co., 165–180.

Brazelton, T.B. and Cramer, B. (1990) *The Earliest Relationship: Parents, Infants, and the Drama of Early Attachment*. Reading, MA: Addison-Wesley Publishing.

Mahler, M., Pine, F., Bergman, A. (1975) *The Psychological Birth of the Human Infant*. New York: Basic Books.

Stern, D. (1985) *The Interpersonal World of the Infant: A View from Psychoanalysis and Developmental Psychology*. New York: Basic Books.

Stern, D. (1995) *The Motherhood Constellation: A Unified View of Parent-Infant Psychotherapy*. New York: Basic Books.

Winnicott, D.W. (1958/1956) Primary maternal preoccupation. In *Collected Papers: Through Paediatrics to Psycho-analysis*. London; Tavistock Publications.

Introduction

Since 1987 when we started our practice, we have had the privilege of getting to know hundreds of mothers, fathers, and babies as they have started their family lives. This early time in the development of a family is a special and sensitive period, marked by growth, change, joy, worry, and overwhelming feelings of love as well as of helplessness. Our work with the Soho Parenting Center has allowed us a window into the complicated, intimate, and wondrous world of family. We have seen relationships emerge, confidences build, and the fabric of each of these new families become a unique pattern—complex, beautiful, strongly bound. During these same years we, too, have begun families and have personally experienced the unique and transforming nature of new parenthood.

Our educational and clinical backgrounds are in the fields of psychology and child and family development. We first met in the Child Life Department of Bellevue Hospital's Outpatient Pediatric Center in New York City. There our work included parent counseling, play psychotherapy for children, and leading groups for adolescent parents. This professional experience as well as our graduate work laid the foundation for our ideas about psychological development and parenting. However, it was our shared experience of being new mothers that really inspired the creation of our parent-counseling service. We provided many things for each other in those early years of motherhood at home with our babies: close companionship, support, and a never-ending, shared interest in the complexities of our new families. We swapped daily concerns, from the most mundane details of baby foods to the largest questions about the impact of our own histories on the emerging identities of our children.

Our deepening friendship as well as our mutual professional interest in therapeutic work with families led us to the decision to start our own mother-infant groups. We began by posting handmade flyers around our New York neighborhood to advertise our first group. We planned to address important issues of infant development as well as to discuss the tremendous impact that motherhood has on a woman's sense of herself. Eight mothers and their babies enrolled and then gathered each week in one of our living rooms over the course of the next two months. From the beginning the group was a great success. It was clear that these women needed to talk about the dramatic changes in their lives: their ideas on the merger of motherhood with work, marriage, sexuality, and friendships as well as about the intricacies of a baby's sleep capabilities, eating patterns, and needs for comfort and play. The ability of this group of women to connect and share their diverse experiences and to feel so helped by the group was inspiring. The idea of a center began to grow, a place where parents could get together and talk, as well as receive guidance from child development professionals. We called it ParenTalk.

On a lead from a colleague at Bellevue Hospital, we approached Drs. Robert Coffey and Marie Keith with the idea of associating our parenting program with their pediatric practice. Coffey and Keith had started working together in 1982. They had quickly become known for their pediatric expertise, for their relaxed approach and supportive advice on parenting. Their small neighborhood practice has grown to be one of the largest in Manhattan. As the four of us talked together at our initial meeting we realized we were each intrigued with the idea of combining medical and psychosocial services. Shortly afterward Drs. Keith and Coffey set us up in the large, open room adjacent to their offices and we started running mother-infant groups for the parents of their pediatric patients. Each year we expanded our program. It now includes mother-infant groups, mother-toddler groups, groups for second-time parents, individual parent counseling, sleep counseling, play therapy for children, long term psychotherapy, and marriage counseling. Parents' responses to these on-site services have been overwhelmingly positive. The stigma and anxiety attached to seeking help of this sort has been greatly reduced by having it available at the pediatricians' offices. It acknowledges that all families will struggle at times and that help from trusted professionals can only serve to enrich and strengthen parents. In 1993 we moved with the Soho Pediatric Group to a new space, which houses their medical offices as well as rooms for our groups and individual work. To reflect our closer affiliation with the Soho Pediatric Group and the expansion of services, ParenTalk became The Soho Parenting Center. Through this unique collaboration of practices, parents have the opportunity to have their needs as a whole family served.

As our practice has developed we have been able to follow those once-upon-a-time babies through their school years. We've seen friendships grow among the mothers in our groups and, wonderfully, among their children as well. We have had the satisfaction of hearing from these women that our mother-infant groups had a profound impact on their early mothering experiences. Our professional practice has grown up. But it really began in our own little circle, the two of us and our firstborn daughters. That circle has grown, incorporating the pasts that created us and spawning other circles that continue to help ease loneliness, share joy, tolerate confusion, understand change, and express love. And when Sandra Kunhardt Basile came to us with the idea for another type of collaboration—the writing of this book—we knew a new circle was about to begin. Sandra has sensitively and exquisitely captured the feeling of our mother-infant groups. Her personal perspective and sensibilities on motherhood have informed the book throughout. Working with a writer who is not only a sister and good friend but also a new mother herself has made our collaboration a rich and intimate one.

We hope *A Mother's Circle* will make you feel less alone, less strange with all the incredible feelings that emerge after the birth of your first baby. We hope it will help you to make sense of your baby's behavior and bolster your confidence as a mother. We hope it will encourage you to join or even to make your own circle of mothers as you find your own style and voice, and that you will bring us with you into that circle.

Jean Kunhardt and Lisa Spiegel

Note to Readers

The women and men in this book are based on real people, real quotes, and real mother-infant groups, but each character is a compilation of many individuals. The names we used in this book are all fictitious. The group represents a sampling of new mothers in the New York metropolitan area. It is meant to speak to all readers, but it is not representative of all mothers. The babies in this book represent average, healthy babies. While *A Mother's Circle* is intended to help you with all sorts of questions you may have about your baby's development, it is not meant in any way to take the place of the advice of the pediatrician who cares for your baby. Having worked predominantly with women, we have chosen to use "mother" to imply the baby's primary caretaker. Fathers, we know, are stepping into that role in greater numbers every day. This book is for them, too.

ONE

Loving Your Baby and the Fear of Spoiling

It is as if a caravan has arrived. One after the next, women stream through the door of the Soho Parenting Center. Each is a new mother carrying a tiny baby. Most of the babies are small enough to be held in pouches or slings, and some are asleep, close to the heartbeat and warmth of their mothers. Each woman also shoulders a bag overflowing with diapers, bottles, blankets, toys, and everything else her baby might need.

Some of the women are flushed as they struggle to remove their coats and scarves and tuck away strollers and other gear while carefully maneuvering their infants. One mother is having particular difficulty. Her baby is crying out in sharp, piercing yelps. The woman is trying to soothe her child by walking and bobbing and singing all at once. She speaks to her baby, "Nell, honey, it's okay. Quiet now." But Nell continues to shriek. Frustration and embarrassment cross the mother's face. She looks self-consciously around the room.

The other women have started to settle themselves in a

circle on the carpeted floor, creating temporary little nests for their infants. Some of the babies lie contentedly on their backs. Some, more active, wave arms and legs in the air. One is nursing. Two sleep, as infants do remarkably well surrounded by noise and activity. Although our offices are a part of their pediatricians' practice, the women do not know one another. Nor do they know us. And our room is a new setting for them. As the mothers greet one another there is some of the shyness that accompanies a new beginning.

The mother with the crying baby orbits the room. Her baby continues to screech. The woman, whose name is Jessica, turns to us now with a look of panic, and says, "I'm sorry. I'm not sure I can stay. Sometimes this goes on for an hour. My doctor says she has colic. My mother says I've spoiled her. I thought she'd be napping during this, but I can never count on anything."

We try to reassure Jessica that we expect that babies will cry during these meetings, that all of our talks are accompanied by the sounds of babies. We encourage her to stay, to walk Nell back and forth while we talk. Jessica agrees, apologizing again, and then turns her attention to her baby.

Over the last eight years we have led well over one hundred mother-infant groups, getting to know more than one thousand new mothers and their babies. Each group has its unique personalities and problems, its own dynamic spark and chemistry, but there are common themes and voices that emerge which connect each group to the next. To observe and participate in the early development of these babies as well as in each woman's unfolding sense of herself as a mother is a profound experience for us. To become aware of the important place these groups hold in the lives of these new mothers has been inspiring. They become a place for humor, support, the breaking down of myths, a place to admit vulnerability, show strength, grow friendships, and share in the delight of watching their babies grow. To watch each group come alive is to witness a new birth.

Carried and bounced for five more minutes, Nell is suddenly quiet and drops off to sleep. Jessica continues to pace the floor for a few minutes. Then she edges closer to the circle of mothers, where she stands and sways, cradling Nell in her arms.

〜ふ THE GROUP

There are nine women in this new mothers' group: Leslie, Marta, Jane, Ronnie, Maggie, Alicia, Elizabeth, Nan, and Jessica. They are between twenty-five and forty years old. All but one are married. Each worked outside of the home before having her baby. A few are back at their jobs, one lost her job, two are still on maternity leave, some will work full-time as mothers. Most are enjoying their babies. Two say they feel almost euphoric. Every mother says the adjustment to motherhood is a challenge and each describes herself as tired.

The babies are between six and eighteen weeks. There are five girls and four boys: Eric, Sarah, Justin, Elyse, Jack, Keith, Lucy, Emma, and Nell. One was adopted, one premature, one unplanned, one seemed a miracle after multiple miscarriages, two were delivered by cesarean section. One of the babies is currently underweight. One has colic. Otherwise, each is healthy and thriving. As described by the mothers, each has her own trademark—sweet, hungry, wide-eyed, happy, cranky, willful, easy, sleepy, or hard to soothe.

∾ WORRY ABOUT SPOILING

Our introductions over, we begin, addressing the group as a whole. "A lot of new mothers fear they are spoiling their babies. And a lot of new mothers are criticized for this. Jessica, you said your mother thinks you have already spoiled Nell. How about the rest of you? Have any of you heard this kind of comment?"

After a whispering chorus of "yesses," Ronnie speaks up. "I couldn't believe it, but the nurse at the hospital where Elyse was born told me I had spoiled my baby after her first night of rooming-in."

"Because of this," says Alicia, holding a pacifier as if it were a piece of court evidence, "I get it from perfect strangers!"

"I was at a party the other day and everyone wanted to hold Emma," says Nan. "I didn't really want to pass her around. A friend of mine said, in a teasing kind of way, that Emma would be spoiled if I didn't let go of her a little."

Mothers often tell us they feel like targets for comments about spoiling. Perhaps the most commonly misused and overused words of so-called wisdom given to a new mother are "Watch out! You'll spoil that baby!" In veiled and not-so-veiled terms, this threat is issued when a mother comforts her crying baby, when she rocks and soothes her to sleep, when she feeds her baby "on demand," when she offers her a pacifier, when she holds her frequently or takes her baby into bed with her. It is as if the mother has crossed a boundary from the domain of good, responsive mothering into that of foolish, even wrongful, overindulgence. People warn: "You'll be sorry!" "You'll pay for that later." "She'll come to expect that." "He'll be a Mama's boy." Or, they say, "She's got you tied around her little finger!" as they wag their own fingers at you.

The women are quiet again and we prompt a little. "Have any of you gotten this message from your partner?"

"I have," says Maggie with a start, half-raising her hand. "My husband tells me that I hold the baby too much. That I have to let him cry or he will be spoiled. I can't bear to let Jack cry, but I'm beginning to feel like maybe I *am* wrong to always pick him up.

"The thing is," Maggie continues, "my husband's parents are of the school that thinks children should be seen and not heard. So I understand why Tom is the way he is. But it frightens me because I'm seeing a side of him I never knew was there before—so strict and withholding. I don't want that for our baby."

"I know what you mean," says Elizabeth. "You don't know what a man is going to be like as a father. It's not a question you ask on your first date: 'So, what are your feelings about child rearing?' "

The group laughs together, Elizabeth's humor helping them to relax as they begin to identify with and support one another.

Alicia adds, "My husband tells me that if I pick Keith up too much, I'm going to make him soft. He says 'He has to be a man!' It's ludicrous! This is a four-month-old baby."

"The reverse is true with us," says Leslie. "Vince, my husband, is the one who can't tolerate the baby crying. Not even for a second. He says I'm too hard on Eric, but I'm afraid that if we go to him all the time, he won't become confident or independent; he won't come into his own."

Very often couples divide on the issue of spoiling— one partner assumes a far more responsive, often reactive, stance in contrast to the other. Most couples have arguments about the type and speed of response, or the need for response to a baby's cry. Superficially, spoiling may seem like a minor concern, but it calls into question feelings about responsibility and negligence, sensitivity and stoicism, dependence and independence, permissiveness and discipline, safety and danger, giving and witholding.

You may be able to deflect unsolicited warnings about spoiling when it comes from the bank teller or a stranger on the bus. But when comments come from someone as close to you as your husband, your mother, or a good friend, they can play on your own insecurities. The apparent logic of their arguments may be hard to debate. And your doubts may spoil your enjoyment of parenting and the spontaneous, natural responses you have to your baby.

We like to watch the relief spread through our groups when we reassure them that they cannot spoil their babies with love and attention, especially during the first year, and that they should feel free to fully indulge and enjoy their babies during this time.

Babies need contact. They need consistent, loving responses to their cries, most especially in the first year of life. So when it comes to loving your baby, you need not hold back. All of your holding, soothing, feeding, rocking, kissing, affection, and attention will not spoil her.

"That feels like a gift," says Nan. "I have wanted to give everything to Emma but wasn't sure if that was really okay."

"I think what you say sounds good in theory," says Leslie to us. "But it seems like responding to their every cry is exactly how we make babies get too dependent. It's important to me that Eric learns how to fend for himself a little bit."

When a mother talks about her new baby's need for self-sufficiency, it usually helps to encourage that mother to think about her own childhood and how her parents dealt with issues of dependence and independence with her. When we pose these thoughts to Leslie she seems initially thrown by our shift in focus and becomes quiet. Then she says, "I *was* very dependent on my parents when I was little. And I was thought of as spoiled and babied, but it was because I needed them so much. I didn't have a lot of confidence, I guess. I remember crying when my mother left me at kindergarten. Maybe that *is* why I want Eric to be more independent. But, won't he learn to expect it if I pick him up every time he cries?"

Babies do learn a lot in their earliest months but not about rewards and manipulation. In this delicate transition period from the womb to the world, babies are learning fundamental, if primitive, lessons about whether this new world is a responsive and nurturing one, about whether or not they have any effect on their environment, about how their needs are met.

"So, picking up Eric when he cries will actually make him *more* confident," says Leslie.

By consistently responding to your baby, not only are

you satisying her needs, you are giving her the important message that she has a voice that brings a response. This sets the earliest foundations of a baby's positive self-esteem and sense of confidence in relation to the world as she knows it. When a baby's cries frequently elicit no response, a vicious cycle of unmet needs and escalating demands can be created. She experiences frustration and a sense of powerlessness. She may later become one of the babies and toddlers who is anxious, fussy, and difficult to soothe. Like everyone else, all babies have social and emotional needs as well as physical and practical ones. They need loving and attention as much as they need milk. They need bodily contact, comfort, and reassurance as much as they need sleep. When an adult soothes a baby, he or she helps that baby to associate human contact with comfort, well-being, and bodily pleasure.

Running these groups for almost a decade has given us the invaluable opportunity to follow a number of mother-child relationships over time. Based on this ongoing involvement, we have had it confirmed for us again and again that those infants whose cries have been responded to by contact and comfort are most often the ones who cry less and demand less attention later in childhood.

"I adopted Sarah and I admit I probably indulge her, but that's what I want to do," says Marta. "Both of my parents have told me that I better be careful not to spoil her. At first I got very defensive. But then I realized that I wanted to be different from my parents anyway and that they are from a totally different generation."

Most of the women in our groups were raised in the fifties and sixties, during the blossoming of the behavioral sciences. Pediatricians and child development experts advised parents at that time to keep babies on strict sched-

ules of feeding and sleeping. The thinking went
something like this: Once a baby was dry and comfortable, had slept and been fed, she should be able to be
content. Cries were to be expected and tolerated; they
were considered good exercise for a baby's lungs. By
going to, picking up, and comforting a crying baby, the
mother was rewarding her baby's crying and was encouraging more of the same. In short order, the baby would
be spoiled.

If your parents warn you not to spoil your baby, it may
be because they were advised in this way. They may have
agreed with this thinking or they may have dutifully followed their pediatrician's suggestions with mixed feelings. The tremendous increase in and new sophistication
of infant development research in the last ten years have
shed new light on the understanding of what babies need.
Although times and the expertise have changed since
your parents were new parents, you too may have mixed
feelings about the concept of spoiling.

✑ RESPONDING AND NURTURING:
0–4 MONTHS

You can assume in the first four months that your baby's
cries mean she is physically uncomfortable. She is hungry,
tired, has a bubble of gas trapped in her belly, she needs
motion or warmth or the right pair of hands to hold her
close. You can feel free to respond, without letting the
fear of spoiling stop you.

"Elyse is a hungry baby and nurses a lot," says Ronnie.
"A lot of people, including my husband, have said, 'She's
always at your breast!' Their mere tone of voice seems to

imply that I'm spoiling Elyse by letting her nurse on demand. I understand why my husband might feel territorial about my body, but why does anyone else care?"

"I know. It's amazing how everyone feels so strongly about it," says Nan. "Everyone tells me *never* to bring Emma into my bed to sleep, as if it were a crime. It's actually the best feeling in the world when I have her in bed with us. But sometimes I wonder if what I'm doing is indulging myself and spoiling Emma."

In the first three to four months feeding on demand is recommended by pediatricians. And choosing to have your baby sleep in bed with you is a natural option, reflective of personal preferences. It is always a good idea to gauge your own needs in relation to your baby's when making decisions about your mothering style, but your relationship with your baby is best when it is *mutually* nurturing and loving. Ronnie and Nan's comments reflect how provocative the mother-infant relationship can be when it comes to such intimate matters as breast feeding and sharing a bed. The intense bond between a mother and child awakens sleeping giants of jealousy in husbands, parents, siblings, and friends.

"Justin is a hungry baby too," says Jane. "Early on I was feeding him every hour or two. Around the clock. So I was constantly asking myself a lot of these questions—was I indulging him or was I doing the right thing? Was feeding on demand making him too demanding? I never thought so, but I had to wonder."

You can assume great latitude and flexibility in the choices you make regarding feeding your baby and her sleeping habits in the first three months. You need not worry about establishing irreversible patterns. Life for a baby is an ever-changing set of stages and a baby's routine is infinitely malleable.

"What about the pacifier?" asks Jane. "I see three-year-olds with their pacifiers and think—uh, oh—I better not let Justin get too attached to one. When my mother sees kids with pacifiers she says, 'I never used a pacifier with *you.*' I guess I've come to see it as a crutch, too."

While feeding on demand and bringing a baby into bed are often appealing to new mothers, giving a baby a pacifier is almost universally mistrusted. Most of the new mothers we meet consider the pacifier an unnecessary, unsightly habit, responsible in part for spoiling a child. Some women say their own mothers' negative feelings about pacifiers have influenced their thinking.

"I had always thought of a pacifier as something a mother used to shut up her baby," says Nan. "But now I'm a real convert. Emma used to nurse for long stretches of time. After the first twenty minutes, it didn't seem like she was hungry. She was just sucking to suck. But I couldn't take it. My cousin suggested giving Emma a pacifier. It took a while for her to get used to it. She'd spit it out. But I kept offering it to her and after about a week she started using it all the time. Now she loves it. I'm happier, too, for that matter."

Sucking is among an infant's most soothing activities, an important way for her to discharge tension and help herself relax. Some babies need to suck more than others. They may nurse for prolonged stretches, suck on their fists, their blankets, their parents' knuckles. Sucking on a pacifier may be a wonderfully comforting, soothing, and necessary activity for your baby.

"Keith is making so many sounds now," says Alicia.

"Sometimes I worry that his pacifier will interfere with that learning."

When the pacifier is overused, becoming a parent's or a caretaker's first response to any noise a baby makes, it *will* eventually interfere with a baby's need to babble and explore. Keep in mind that most babies' needs for a pacifier will naturally diminish at around four to five months, long before a baby is forming words.

"I feel like a human pacifier," says Maggie. "My arms may be about to break, but Jack cries when I put him down. He seems to need me to hold him or rock him constantly. But he's ten weeks now, and sometimes I do worry that I'm spoiling him."

Just as some babies need to suck, some babies need lots of body-to-body contact. They frequently need to be held close and for prolonged periods of walking and rocking. If your baby is like this, by all means hold her as much as you want to or can. You may find it helpful to carry her in a front pack, even indoors, to free your hands and keep the close contact she needs. Just as with a baby's sucking urge, this need diminishes with time and soon your baby will be capable of more independence. In the meantime if *you* want more freedom of movement, you can put your baby in an infant seat or swing to see how she fares. Stay close by at first so it does not seem like a dramatic transition. With time you can gradually increase her tolerance for this kind of independence.

Some babies also need body-to-body contact to fall asleep. We tell parents that for the first three to four months anything goes regarding sleep. You can rock or nurse your baby to sleep, let her sleep in a stroller, or with you in bed, without fear of "spoiling."

"I worry that I'm not playing with Elyse enough," says

Ronnie. "When I'm not nursing her, it seems like I spend most of my time trying to get chores done."

"I know what you mean," says Jane. "There's not as much time to play as I thought there would be. It seems like I'm either nursing Justin or doing the laundry. And then my mother comes over and lavishes gifts on Justin. She adores him. I think it is her objective to spoil him."

Finding a balance between the endless chores of motherhood and the tender moments of one-on-one play and direct interaction with your baby is an art, one that is developed with time. Sometimes a baby will cry because she is bored, because she needs company, stimulation, something new to look at. However, a baby does not need constant, formal entertainment nor a wealth of toys. She has an innate drive to learn about her world and will be stimulated by whatever you are doing: by the sound of your voice, by lights, colors, and movements, by the overhead fan in your bedroom, by the sunlight and wind out of doors, by the aisles of food at the grocery store. If your baby is content to come along for the ride, you can relax and feel confident that she is stimulated enough. Of course one-on-one, face-to-face play is an important way of connecting with your baby and should make up a part of every day.

The Need to Cry

Babies cry. For them, it is as natural as sleeping or eating and is a part of their limited repertoire of activities. At two weeks a baby's crying will increase as she wakes up to the world. And then this will decrease again sometime around the eighth to tenth week as she develops more interests. Very generally speaking, babies will cry for about two hours a day. Whan a baby wakes and cries out, it is alright to let her cry a little bit before immediately offering milk. In this way you can identify what kind of crying it is. We do not advocate letting your baby cry without going to her, but small amounts of fussing can sometimes actually help her discharge tension and energy.

Sometimes your baby will cry and you will not be able to soothe her. She won't nurse, take a bottle, sleep, watch a mobile, quiet to hear you sing. She won't suck on her pacifier or your finger. She won't be soothed by the bouncing walk that always works. You've tried everything in your repertoire and still your baby is miserable. If this describes a routine that is familiar to you, your baby may have reached her limit for sensory input. She is overstimulated. Her cries may be, in effect, a last-ditch effort to block out stimulation. If you think this is the case, you can put her in her crib and let her cry, within earshot, for up to ten minutes. Her cries may sound particularly frantic but then she may quickly settle herself or fall to sleep, in which case you can assume she was indeed overstimulated.

"I think I discovered that by accident," says Leslie. "It's an amazing thing. It had been a long day. Eric was cranky and wouldn't stop crying. I was just barely holding on, waiting for my husband to come home. Then—guess what?—Vince called to say he would be late. I was so exhausted I couldn't think straight and Eric's cries were getting me crazy. So I put him in his bassinette and went and took a shower to wake up. In less than three minutes Eric stopped crying. I got out of the shower immediately and went to check on him. There I was dripping wet and he was fast asleep. I was surprised but really relieved to see that he had settled himself."

Hard-to-Soothe Babies

In almost every one of our groups there is a baby who has colic or is especially hard to soothe. Regardless of whether she is bottle or breast fed, she may be gassy, supersensitive to stimulation, or generally uncomfortable. She may cry continuously throughout the day or be irritable every night for a period of several hours.

"Jessica, you mentioned that your mother said you're spoiling your baby. What has that been like for you?"

"My mother has never experienced a baby with colic and, in her defense, I think it *is* hard to understand. No one really does. You can't imagine it until you've lived with it. But my mother is convinced I'm only making matters worse and that I'm spoiling Nell," Jessica answers in a quiet voice.

"My pediatrician assures me that Nell is the way she is because she is uncomfortable," Jessica continues. "She says it has nothing to do with how I am treating her. But sometimes I think my mother is right. I think Nell has gotten used to constant attention from me. She screams for hours sometimes. I'll hold her and bounce her and she stops for a minute but then starts screaming again. I'll rub her belly and she stops crying for a minute and then she'll start right back up, needing more."

It may appear that Jessica is catering to Nell's every whim and whimper, or that she is not good at mothering because she is unable to console her baby, or even that Nell is a "bad" baby because she cries so much. But colic is neither a personality trait, nor learned or "spoiled" behavior. It is physiological discomfort.

Mothers of fussy, uncomfortable infants tend to worry a lot about spoiling because their babies require enormous amounts of attention and soothing. A colicky or a high-need baby can make a woman doubt her capacity as a mother and question her maternal love, to say nothing of pushing her toward sanity's edge. We ask Jessica how she is coping with Nell's constant demands and if she has any help with the baby.

"I wasn't prepared for this," Jessica responds, her shoulders slumping. "I never anticipated needing someone to help me take care of my baby. My husband's been helpful, but I think he's reached his limit. And really, he's not around that much. My pediatrician has been supportive. And then, I guess I thought this group would help. But in a way it's shocking to see how easygoing these other babies are. It makes me think I must be doing something wrong." Jessica's eyes fill with tears.

"My heart goes out to you, Jessica. I know a little of what you are going through," says Maggie. "Sometimes Jack will cry for an hour at the end of the day and it's the worst feeling in the world not to be able to help him. By the end of his crying I'm ready to cry myself."

Colic throws a monkey wrench in the whole business of soothing a baby and often in the adjustment to motherhood. It is normal for a mother of a high-need baby to feel upset, concerned, and frustrated as well as guilty, angry, and disappointed. It is natural for her to compare her baby with others, to worry about her baby and about how her baby's persistent crying reflects on her. It is common for her to feel different from other mothers, envious of the comparatively easy relationship between a comfortable baby and her less stressed mother. Usually it is not enough to assure her that there is a wide range of "normal" behavior in young babies, even in a small group such as ours.

We urge Jessica not to continue trying to go it alone. We have found that when a baby has colic, her mother typically finds it near-impossible to leave her baby with someone else. She figures she is the only one who could endure her baby's continual crying in a loving manner. But very often mothers of colicky babies experience exhaustion and defeat which sometimes can be followed by depression. Jessica needs to let her husband know just how hard it is for her. Together they can make arrangements for Jessica to have some time off, to get out of the house, to refuel. Nell's colic should pass in another four to six weeks. And when it does, life will change dramatically.

A Mother's Needs

"Lucy's been fairly easy to take care of," says Elizabeth. "But even with an *easy* baby I'm stricken with the idea that life as I knew it is over."

It is common for a woman to feel trapped during the first months at home with her baby, especially when motherhood comes fast on the heels of a full and varied work life. Assuming the primary role in the intense and demanding relationship with a new baby can even feel oppressive at times. Add to this the premise that a baby cannot be spoiled in the first year and you may feel stretched beyond your capacity to give. But being a responsive parent doesn't mean giving one hundred percent of yourself one hundred percent of the time. You have needs, too, and natural limits to your time and energy. Getting someone to help you with your baby even one afternoon a week so that you can have a break can go a long way toward making your life easier and more enjoyable. It may also ultimately help you to give more freely to your baby.

We have said that no amount of loving, responding, and attention giving is too much. By this we do not mean to imply that you should never let your baby cry for short periods of time without responding. There will be moments when you can't respond to your baby right away, when you are having an important telephone call or finishing a shower. This is not neglect. It is life, and life has its frustrations. Even for babies. But frustration is not always as negative as you may think.

～ HELPING YOUR BABY TOLERATE FRUSTRATION: 4–12 MONTHS

Alicia's baby Keith is lying on a blanket on the floor. He drops his toy. It rolls in front of us with a jingle of bells, just out of Keith's reach. He turns and wriggles to get it. At nineteen weeks, Keith is a perfect example of the changing needs and capacities of this age. He is beginning to use his body in new ways, and with each new wiggle learns what he can reach for. As he tries to get his toy, he illustrates how frustration can also serve as motivation. It would not spoil Keith to retrieve his toy for him, but it might be to his advantage in other ways not to respond right away. Small amounts of frustration can be productive incentives for a baby to develop and grow. Too much can be overwhelming. If Alicia can wait and watch Keith, she can assess his potential and his needs before deciding how to respond.

It is common for a mother to continue doing what has always worked to keep her baby happy. But early patterns quickly become outdated. Babies eventually stop needing to be swaddled, rocked to sleep, fed every few hours, stop needing for you to rush over and rescue them. As a baby develops the ability for some independence, she also learns to tolerate minor frustrations and delays. She will begin to stretch herself to learn new physical abilities and verbal sounds. She will discover techniques for self-soothing, such as sucking on a blanket, twirling a lock of hair, holding a beloved object, or rolling over into a comfortable position in her crib. She will be able to go for longer times between feedings. She acquires the capacity to sleep through the night.

"Now that Keith is a little older it's easier to know when I have to respond quickly," says Alicia. "All of his cries used to sound the same to me. Now I recognize differences. Recently he's been making this funny little forced cry with a half smile on his face. Then I know it's not so urgent."

As your baby's abilities change, so must your expectations of her abilities. To encourage independent play, a few times a day you can let your baby sit in an infant seat or lie on a mat on the floor with toys. If she is capable of simple contentment and independent play for a short period, you can gradually extend this.

As babies begin to inch on their bellies, crawl, pull up, stand up, take their first steps, climb stairs, and venture out, they also begin to get bumps and bruises, to totter and fall, to scrape and cut themselves. A parent may wonder where to draw the line between overprotectiveness, which might be construed as "babying" or "spoiling," and taking the necessary precautions to keep a baby from hurting herself.

It is imperative that you make your baby's environment

safe to move around in and explore. It is also important to begin to teach your baby what is acceptable behavior and what is not. But if you constantly hover, or consistently say "no," or if you gasp with alarm each time she falls, she may begin to think the world is not a safe place. Babies respond strongly to their parent's sense of fear and caution. When a parent allows a baby to practice walking, for example, to pick herself up after a minor spill, the child learns to take these bumps more in stride.

When a baby is hurt, frightened, or upset, she needs you to go to her without hesitation. But for the many occasions during a baby's day when she makes a protest or a demand, try not to respond as if she has no capacity to wait. Now, as you fix a bottle, she can watch you and anticipate satisfaction. If she becomes impatient and cries out, talk to her, sing and clap, tell her you are on your way, explain to her what you are doing. Typically, babies do not develop language until past their first birthday, but they can understand a lot of words and messages before age one. These "conversations" are the building blocks of communication.

Early Limit Setting

While we believe that a child cannot be spoiled during the first year, limits, even those before the first birthday, are important. You are probably already setting them, without even knowing it. When your baby innocently pulls her father's chest hairs or swipes at your face with sharp fingernails, or bites you while nursing, the very change in the tone of your voice when you say "Ouch!" conveys a message of displeasure. Then when you add "Gentle, gentle!" or "No, no!" this introduces the concept of limits. Over time your baby internalizes these every-day lessons.

"I've heard that it's important to avoid the word 'No,' " says Marta. "If I don't say 'No' then maybe Sarah won't learn to use it or throw it back in my face."

More helpful than the word "No" by itself is an explanation such as "Hot!" or "Ouch!" or "You have to be gentle." You can then add "No, no," so your baby makes the association.

"What about children who *are* spoiled?" asks Marta. "I just spent a day with some friends who have a three-year-old who is, well, a spoiled brat. I'd hate for Sarah to turn out like that."

The image of a spoiled child is a dreaded one. Usually the picture is of a toddler or preschooler who demands and whines and insists, who kicks and pouts, who knows just how to push her parents' buttons, how to manipulate and cajole, be it for sweets, presents, television, or her own way. Disrespectful, often aggressive, she can't listen, can't take no for an answer, can't wait, can't share.

It is hard to know if the little girl with whom Marta spent the day is, in fact, a "spoiled" child. All children go through difficult periods as they grow. All children will appear spoiled at some point. Stages when a child has difficulty waiting and sharing, when she is especially clingy, whiny, and demanding are all typical of normal child development. However, chronically demanding, objectionable, whiny behavior usually indicates either that a child has received far less attention than she needs or that she has never been stretched in her ability to wait, to use her own resources, or to soothe herself.

"Limit setting is going to be hard for me," says Marta. "My parents were very strict. There were so many rules and things I couldn't do as a child. I remember having to stay in my room for hours once because I broke a candy bowl. And it was an accident. But my parents didn't seem to care about my side of the story or how I was feeling. I never want Sarah to feel controlled or misunderstood that way."

Marta's conflict is not an uncommon one. She wants only to befriend her child. She fears spoiling but is anxious about setting limits. She sees discipline and authority as punitive and mean but realizes they have their place. Having felt restricted, misunderstood, and unfairly reprimanded as a child, she wishes to offset her baby's frustration and anger with understanding and permissiveness. How Marta experienced her parents—as strict rather than lenient, as witholding rather than giving—affects how she is with her baby. Marta's parents put a heavy emphasis on rules and obedience, and in reaction Marta wants to be completely in tune with her baby's feelings and desires.

The need and demand for you to set limits for your child will come more into play when she is older, but your feelings about this are integral to your parenting style from the start. There will come a point at which true limit setting begins. And it is not far off. Having mastered walking, a baby's main mission in life seems to be simply to destroy. She will put everything into her mouth, climb up onto places from which she cannot get down, and pull everything within reach onto the floor.

When the time comes, many parents have difficulty being firm about setting limits, especially with older children. More psychologically minded than their own parents, the current generation wants to be sensitive to their babies' needs and feelings and nurturing to their children's egos. But loving and limit setting are not mutually exclusive. You can be a close, loving, devoted parent and a figure of authority at the same time. When used judiciously, saying "No" will not crush your child's spirit. In fact, limits are critical for her sense of security and self-worth. Limits do not simply shut a door. They stretch a child, teach her about the world, and let her know she is protected. Limits also help a child to learn about self-control, respect, and empathy for others. They are a necessary and important part of parenting.

"I was visiting a friend whose two-and-a-half-year-old boy wanted a cookie," says Jessica. "His mother gave him one. Then the boy asked for another. His mother gave him another. When the boy asked for a third cookie, his mother said no. The child cried for almost half an hour. I couldn't stand it. I know I won't be able to do that with Nell. I'm afraid I'll give in just to avoid that kind of upset and anger—on her part *and* mine."

It can be frightening and upsetting to have your baby get angry or cry out because of something you impose or withhold. In fact, one of the most difficult challenges a parent faces is tolerating a child's discomfort—be it illness, fatigue, pain, frustration, disappointment, or anger. It will not always be possible, or even advisable, to take away those feelings. But it will be important for you as parent to let your child express these feelings and to recognize and respond to them. Your baby's consistent experience of your attempt to understand her needs is critically important to her sense of self and of relationships.

"My father spoiled me," says Jane. "But I say that with pride and affection. He indulged me. But it wasn't really with material things. It was with his time. He talked with me. We took walks together. He brought me to his office.

He was strict about some things. But I know he adored me."

The definitions of "baby" when used as a verb include coddle, indulge, pamper, and spoil. But to baby a baby is only natural. As your baby grows in the first year, you will be constantly shifting between soothing her and testing, between welcoming her neediness and encouraging her independence. The tension between your needs and your baby's needs, between giving yourself over to the baby and holding back ever so slightly for her sake will affect your approach to many areas of parenting. You will see it in your style of feeding your baby, of getting her to sleep, as well as in your decisions about staying home or returning to the workplace.

How parents feel about the concept of spoiling can be seen as a metaphor for their relationship with their babies. It touches on issues from learning how to soothe your baby to letting your baby learn to soothe herself. It reflects your own style of parenting as you learn to love and to set limits at the same time. The fear of spoiling may rob you of life's true pleasures with your new baby—rocking or nursing your baby to sleep, hugging, holding, and soothing her. This is just the beginning of a long and loving relationship, but infancy and babyhood are the times when parents can most freely baby their babies. It passes quickly.

TWO

Work and Motherhood
Challenges and Choices

It is a bright fall afternoon. The new mothers arrive with red cheeks, their babies bundled up in extra layers. A few of the women remember each others' names. A few make introductions again. As we sit down together, comments circle about how Keith has grown, how Lucy did with her three-month shots, how Jessica survived her week with Nell. Then, over gurgles and cries and the hushing sound of a shaking rattle, we introduce our subject for discussion: work.

Work is a pressing, complicated, often heart-wrenching issue for new mothers. Will you stay at home with your baby? Will you go back to your job? Will you try to do a little of both? Will your husband take on a role at home with the baby? It may all seem like a simple question, one of finances and inclinations. But it is not. Your answer encompasses a whole range of issues—from how you were brought up to your aspirations in the world.

No matter what you end up doing—returning to your job, working part-time, or taking on the care of your baby full-time—there will be some conflict in your heart. It may help you to know you have company. Lots of it. Almost every new mother struggles with opposing urges. It may take months or even years to sort out your dual roles and to find the right balance.

During your pregnancy or the adoption process, you probably made a plan about whether or when you would return to work. Once your baby is born, this plan may progress as you had thought it would or it may feel surprisingly wrong. Going back to work may feel unexpectedly difficult. Or, full-time mothering may not be what you had imagined. For many, a period of indecision sets in, one marked by confusion, guilt, and longing. The ensuing decision-making process is unquestionably difficult but it can also be one of discovery as you learn about your new baby and your new role. Our objective is to help you sift through your expectations and goals about both work and motherhood, to alert you to potential stumbling blocks and help you to make the best decision for you and your family. Keep in mind that compromise is inevitable. The process by its nature compels you to confront your ambitions and your husband's, to accept limitations, to take on new goals and create some balance in your new life.

The women are eager to tell their stories. Leslie, laid-off from her computer programming job when she was six months pregnant, is collecting unemployment and has filed a discrimination suit. Although she is still upset about losing her job, she admits that she was relieved to have had the decision about work made for her and is enjoying the time with her baby. Leslie's husband, Vince, is supportive of Leslie being home full-time but feels nervous about being the only breadwinner. Leslie plans to look for a new job eventually, but for now her unemployment payments are helping to offset some of the couple's new expenses.

Marta is a single parent. She has no choice but to continue working. She likes her job at a social service agency but is exhausted from juggling full-time work with motherhood and is having a hard time making ends meet. She says that the hardest parts are never having time for herself and not having someone on whom she can totally rely. She is pleased, however, with the day care she found for her daughter.

Jessica is troubled. Two years earlier she had returned to college to finish her undergraduate studies. While there she fell in love, got married, and became pregnant. Only four credits short of earning her degree, she again put her education on a back burner, this time to devote herself to family life. But Nell has colic, Jessica's husband is retreating into his work, and, feeling overwhelmed, Jessica now finds herself questioning her decisions.

Alicia went back to work after a six-week maternity leave. She feels confident about the full-time nanny she and her husband chose to care for Keith. Alicia tells us that she is happier as a busy lawyer than as a full-time mother. She misses Keith during the day but loves her time with him in the mornings, evenings, and on weekends.

Nan worked as a photo stylist for a big retail company. Her pregnancy was unplanned. Even though she was flourishing at her job, Nan knew the long hours and fast pace of her work would not mix well with motherhood.

She worked out a three-month maternity leave but is not convinced she could ever go back to work full-time. Still, she doesn't want to lose her career entirely. And Nan's husband has been pressuring her to get back on her career track. For the meantime, Nan is keeping in touch with her colleagues and is doing some work on a very part-time basis.

Elizabeth, a publicity agent, also wasn't sure how she would feel about working once the baby arrived. She proposed a six-month leave of absence from work and got it. She and her husband agree they would like to try to juggle their careers with parenthood, sharing in the care of Lucy. Elizabeth and her boss have put together a plan in which Elizabeth will work part-time from her apartment and part-time out of the company's office. Jonathan is planning to cut back to a four-day workweek when Lucy is six months old. One day a week he will be full-time at home with Lucy. When Lucy is one he will be home with her two days a week.

Jane, an office manager, and Ronnie, an elementary school teacher, each stopped working and are feeling good about their decisions to be full-time mothers. Jane projects that she will devote herself to mothering for at least five years. She is focusing her energies on her baby and on creating a new life for her family within the community. Ronnie projects that she will be at home with her baby for at least two years.

Maggie, who owns and runs a restaurant with her husband, is in the throes of an argument with him about when she will return to work. She wants to stay home with the baby for another three months. He wants her to go back to work immediately.

Each of the women in the group is grappling with the

dilemmas about work which all mothers face today. As they unravel their stories they also begin to knit together their old lives with their new lives.

✧ YOUR IDENTITY AND YOUR JOB

Elizabeth speaks first. "I don't know who I am anymore. I reach for my briefcase and—Zap—I find a diaper bag. It's like Cinderella in reverse."

Even though she manages a sense of humor, Elizabeth is anxious about her waning sense of identity. She adores her baby and being a mother, but she misses her work and her life at the office. She is uncertain what her priorities should be and even about how she feels. She looks forward to the time when Jonathan is more involved with Lucy's care. In preparation for her upcoming part-time status at work, she has started to send Lucy, her twelve-week-old, to day care two mornings a week. On those two mornings she is plagued with guilt.

Alicia, a real estate lawyer, back at her job, has a different brand of guilt.

"I don't feel guilty about leaving Keith with a nanny. I feel guilty that I *don't* feel guilty. But the truth is, it's impossible for me to conceive of staying home with the baby. I'm almost forty. I've been working since college. I adore Keith and I think he's more important than anything else, but I'm more career-oriented than mother-oriented. The thing is I'm more confident as a career person. I *know* I'm a good lawyer. I'm not so sure I'm a good mother."

Jane, who quit her job as an office manager to be a full-time mother, responds to Alicia's commitment to her profession.

"When I see you dressed up in your work clothes it makes me miss my old life. I know I want to be home with my baby, but I'm also envious of your professional life. Five months ago I was consumed by my job. I don't want it back, but these days *my* biggest challenge is getting Justin to sleep at night."

The generation of women now in their twenties, thirties, and forties was raised to pursue careers, to break out of the mold of woman-as-wife-and-mother. Now these same women are becoming mothers. It can take a long time to adjust, and during the first year of motherhood many women experience a crisis about who they are. In truth, it is hard to even imagine the profound changes a baby brings. We have found that most women have mixed feelings about what they want. Even women like Alicia, who knew she would go back to work, and Jane, who always wanted to stay home, experience some confusion and sadness about their choices.

Marta says, "I guess we are all a little tortured."

Swept up in the anticipation of the new baby, few mothers-to-be give due credit to the role of work in their lives. After a month or two away from her job, however, the new mother can better appreciate how much her life had been built around it. If you are wondering why staying home with your new baby makes you feel lost instead of found, think about how a job provides the framework to life. It is why you get up when you do, why you buy the clothes you wear, how you spend most of your waking hours, perhaps why you live where you do. Salary influences lifestyle; work defines free time. The rewards of a job that you *like* are many. It can be stimulating and challenging, creative and involving, vital to your sense of self. Work provides financial independence and a community of colleagues. It can become, over time, a stabilizing force in life. Your workplace may provide you with friends and a social life. What you do for a living is often the first thing you will be asked about yourself when meeting new people. In some important ways, work defines who you are.

Alicia says, "After my second week at home with Keith, I said to myself, 'I need to go back to work. I miss the structure.'"

Jessica has been listening intently while bouncing fussing Nell on her knees.

"I've been thinking the same thing. I've got to get out of the house. Sometimes I think I'm going out of my mind."

Alicia's and Jessica's reactions are not uncommon. New to their roles, life feels topsy-turvy, out of control. A lot of women decide to go back to work during the early months of motherhood. In fact, these early months require a big adjustment, and if your baby is hard to soothe, they can be a tremendous trial. After the third month, life at home with a baby becomes more settled. You will begin to feel more sure of yourself as a mother and will be able to see more clearly what your decisions regarding work imply for you.

Jessica concurs. "I didn't expect I'd feel this way, but if someone asked me right now to decide between school full-time or mothering full-time, I'd say . . . school!"

Elizabeth protests. "But that's like asking a woman in labor if she's going to have another baby!"

Coming to terms with what best suits you over the long run is an important first step in the decision-making process. Do you find enjoyment in the pleasures and challenges of being with your baby, in the slowed-down day, in domestic life? Do you enjoy managing the household, making nearly all of the decisions for your baby? Do you thrive on the challenges of your job, on intellectual stimulation or on companionship with peers? Is management or being a part of a community or producing something necessary to your sense of self? Are you filled with pride at your decision or with guilt? Is your decision your own or were you pressured into it? These are just some of the questions you might ask yourself as you begin to sort out your priorities. Early motherhood is a time of enormous internal change and growth. Once your baby is born everything seems different—your picture of yourself, your ambitions, your feelings about work, about your husband, your parents, your baby, your past, and your future.

〜 VOICES

"My boss has always encouraged me to pursue my work and that's my choice," says Alicia. "But the other day, right in front of me, he said to a colleague in a jocular tone of voice, 'I'd never let *my* wife work this late. She'd be home with the kids.' I think it was about six-thirty! I've never heard the mixed message so clearly."

New mothers are bombarded with mixed messages from colleagues, bosses, relatives, friends, and neighbors. Some women internalize these opinions until they hear conflicting voices in their own heads. One voice says, "Achieve! Be successful!" while the other says "A good mother stays home."

"I've only been home with the baby for two months,"

says Nan. "But I know some of my working friends think that I'm being indulgent."

Staying at home as a full-time mother has some of the trappings of indulgence. You may stay in your pajamas until midday but only because you haven't had time to shower. You may watch television after lunch but mostly to hear the sound of another adult voice. Some people may imagine you cooing with your baby all day, taking lazy walks in the park, and napping in the afternoons. But for all the pleasures that you do get from mothering full-time, the reality of your day is around-the-clock work. When a mother is labeled "indulgent" after only two months at home with her baby, it is clear that the social pressure to return to work is high. To make it more confusing, another woman might be labeled "indulgent" if she chose to go back to her career.

Sometimes it is easier to feel pushed into a decision about your work life, absolved of the responsibility. While it may be difficult not to be affected by other people's judgments and expectations, it behooves you to find out what is right for you. It can be an unfamiliar exercise to decipher what your own feelings are, to uncover your own voice. For now, try to get at the hidden translations in your own reasonings.

"I have to go back to work. We need the money," may translate into "My husband is nervous about money."

"It would feel awful to leave my baby with someone else all day," may translate into "My mother devoted her life to me."

"I can't imagine walking away from my career," may translate into "My boss depends on me. He expects me back. I don't have a choice." Or even, "My parents sacrificed so I could have a good education and a good career. I want to fulfill their hopes for me."

"My job is too good to let go," may translate into "My friends think my job is too good to let go."

Sometimes women convince themselves that their decision is the only right one and then unwittingly alienate mothers who are juggling differently. Often women secretly envy the choices made by other mothers. Unspoken rivalries exist between mothers who work outside the home and those who are at home full-time with their babies. During the course of our discussions it becomes clear that every choice brings some brand of conflict and that everyone is making compromises. The women take some comfort in the fact that there is no single or perfect solution.

∽ LIFE AT HOME: THE EARLY MONTHS

"I'm supposed to go back to work at the restaurant but my mind has been so scattered I can't imagine being able to do that job anymore," says Maggie, rocking her baby in her arms. "I can barely carry on an adult conversation. I forget things all the time and I feel like my brain is in a fog."

"I know what you mean," says Leslie. "And, it's not only forgetting things, it's forgetting how to be social. I'm afraid I'm not interesting anymore. I have no interest in reading the paper. I only talk about the baby. Even my husband says it's getting a bit much. I shudder to think what I would do at a dinner party."

Almost every new mother of the hundreds we've worked with has been concerned about what they describe as a growing inability to think clearly. Many deride themselves for not being able to finish sentences, for leaving errands half-done, for forgetting appointments, for becoming obsessed with baby things to the exclusion of adult interests. Because this phenomenon is not formally addressed in parenting books, some new mothers become truly alarmed.

Elizabeth, now officially the comedienne of the group, announces, "I've heard the brain gets expelled with the placenta!"

The women are laughing. But hearing one another describe the same "fog brain" phenomenon comes as an enormous relief. If you have been feeling as if your brain were on hold and have wondered if this was a permanent state, don't worry. It's not.

Mothering requires functions of the brain not generally used in the workplace or office; it demands that you be more instinctual and emotional, less logical and linear in your thinking. Communication with your baby at this stage is more physical and emotional than verbal. From the first day of your new baby's life, you are learning how to read your baby's sign language, the subtle innuendoes and the not-so-subtle cries of his infant behavior. In addition to this entirely new orientation and way of interacting, sleep deprivation takes its toll on your ability to think clearly. So, give yourself some credit. You are hard at work learning about your baby and about yourself as a mother. And take heart; with time, your faster, more logical way of processing and verbalizing will return.

For some women, becoming a mother and staying home with a baby can be a respite from the job scene, its pressures and stresses, its politics and competitiveness.

"The career issues melt away when I'm nursing my baby or when he smiles at me," says Leslie with a satisfied look in her eyes.

Ronnie chimes in. "Work pales in comparison with being a mother."

After a marked pause, Maggie says, "I'm almost embarrassed to say this, but it's not been that easy for me. I feel like it's a huge adjustment."

Life at home can also have its stresses and pressures. In fact, the old adage, "A woman's work is never done" has a lot of truth in it. You may also be discovering that a *mother's* work is never seen. Life dissolves into countless, consuming routines, nurturing acts and invisible chores: changing diapers, changing clothes, changing crib sheets, nursing, burping, cleaning spit-up, bathing, swaddling, rocking, soothing, singing, smiling, cooing, not to mention grocery shopping, cooking, keeping house, and doing the laundry. Entire days go by with little to show for them except, perhaps, a messy house.

"Everything in my life is slippery," says Leslie. "I can't get ahold of it. The apartment, for instance. We used to have a clean, ordered apartment. Now I go from room to room and there is stuff everywhere. The problem is I start something, the baby cries, and I leave it and I may never get back to it. It might sound trivial, but it makes my *life* seem so messy."

Now everyone in the group begins to talk at once. Life is a little out of control, they agree, and a messy apartment or house symbolizes just that.

"When my husband comes home from work and asks me what I did that day, I can't come up with anything much," says Nan. "Meanwhile the house looks like a bomb hit it and I'm tired and bitchy. The funny thing is, even *I* can't figure out where the days go."

Ronnie picks up where Leslie leaves off. "I told *my* husband not to ask anymore what I did that day. It's just a conversation opener, I know, but it was making me so pissed off."

Maggie, whose work life revolved around the social setting of a restaurant, sees motherhood as particularly isolating.

"I do love being with Jack, but it's such a quiet existence. I was used to constant social interaction at work. My whole lifestyle has changed."

"One of the hardest adjustments for me has been the sudden isolation I feel as a new mother," says Ronnie. "Not only did I give up my job, but I'm the first one of my friends to have a baby and they aren't interested in talking about baby stuff. By the time David gets home at night I'm practically in tears I'm so desperate to talk."

"It's definitely an adjustment," Jane agrees, "but as I get used to it, I think I may never want to go back to a job again."

"It feels right to me to be with my baby all the time, too," Maggie returns. "But there are so many romantic notions about motherhood! Some days my biggest challenge is simply coping. I consider it an accomplishment when I take a shower or do a load of laundry."

Motherhood is not just a new job, it's a new way of life. It can be exhilarating one moment and humbling the next. It is emotionally rich but it can also be exhausting, boring, and isolating. Though the actual tasks of mothering may seem repetitive and unimportant, the role you play is an endlessly creative and hugely important one.

Being with your baby, showing him the world, consistently comforting and nurturing him and structuring his life is a monumental job and achievement.

～ CHOICES AND GUILT

Guilt is an occupational hazard of motherhood. A nagging sense of it accompanies most mothers on whatever path they choose. You may feel guilt at the anger and frustration you have toward your baby after a long day at home with him, guilt at the half-baked job you think you are doing both at home and at work, guilt at the relief you feel when you return to the office.

Guilt will crop up at the most unexpected moments and places. Alicia describes herself as committed to her career and clear about the fact that she would be unfulfilled at home with her baby. But one day, Keith gets sick. Alicia leaves work to take Keith to the pediatrician.

"When the nanny called me at the office I could hear Keith crying. He sounded so miserable. Luckily I could take the time and that's what I wanted to do, so I was feeling good about myself, very maternal. But when the doctor asked me what Keith's bowel movements had been like in the past twenty-four hours I had to say 'I really don't know.' It was a horrible moment. I was overcome with guilt."

Many of the mothers in our groups who are considering a return to work have guilt in their hearts before they have even made a decision. They express a desperate need to know what is "best" for their babies. They ask us what is the optimal age to leave a baby and return to work. They want to know what is the optimal child care choice.

They wonder if day care can compromise a child's development in any way. They are disappointed and sometimes even angry when they hear there are no hard-and-fast rules governing this choice.

No matter how liberated, most women believe somewhere in their hearts that they should not leave their baby to someone else's care. The image of a mother who is devoted to her children all day and all night is deeply embedded in our culture. No decision will be guilt-free. To some extent, guilt is something you may have to live with. Or even to learn from on occasion.

In the best of all possible worlds mothers and/or fathers would be able to be home with their babies for substantial amounts of time during their children's early years. But in the real world, social and economic pressures, coupled with a woman's ability and desire to find herself in the workplace, conflict with this ideal. Trying to find a balance between what is best for your baby, for you, and your family is a big job in itself.

What's best for your baby and what's best for you are intertwined. How you experience stress and how you feel about yourself is critical to your relationship with your baby. If staying home and not returning to your job causes you great frustration or unhappiness, you may not be able to engage effectively with your baby as a result. If returning to work and sharing the care of your baby with your husband or with someone else leaves you with a pervasive sense of missing out, that too will affect your relationship with your baby. What becomes most important is that you be able to live with your decision comfortably. It is to no one's benefit to knock yourself out to make something work that feels fundamentally wrong to you.

The primary attachment between mother and child continues to grow under many different conditions. Working parents can and do maintain healthy, loving, and strong relationships with their babies. Never underestimate your baby's capacity to love. Or your own.

∿ HIDDEN AGENDAS AND YOUR OWN HISTORY

"I'm fortunate," Ronnie says, "because I don't have to go back to work. My husband is something of a workaholic but I can't say I have that problem. Eventually I want to figure out a way to make money again, but not in the typical nine-to-five job. For now, I'm doing what I've always wanted to."

Many women find deep satisfaction in the nurturing role of motherhood. A child creates new priorities and new ambitions for them. Ronnie epitomizes this satisfaction. Some of the women in the group express envy at how Ronnie can accept and enjoy this role without conflict. Wanting to learn more, we ask Ronnie about the role models she grew up with, and what her mother did.

"My mother was a nurse. She stopped working to be a mother. And then she went back to her career after we were all in grade school. I was the oldest, so she was home until I was about twelve. I'm sure that's why I want to be home with Elyse. I can't imagine doing anything else. When Mom went back to work she had some night shifts and my father helped out at home. That was kind of neat. I remember cooking supper with him two nights a week. But no matter what her work schedule was, Mom always made us feel loved. I talk to her much more on the phone than I used to. It's funny because now she's working and I'm home."

"My mother worked before she had children, too," says Nan. "She was devoted to us. You would have thought she was the typical, traditional wife and mother. But before us, she had been a costume designer for the theater. And a good one. She gave it up to raise me and my brother and sister. Even though I know she chose to, there must have been a great sadness in giving up her own art, her own success. Especially since it was such a fun world. I wish I had asked her more about it. She died four years ago. But until I had Emma I never really understood what it meant to make those choices. I love my work, but I want to be there for Emma."

"I know what you mean," says Maggie. "I want my baby to feel secure that I'm his mother and that he's loved and I know it's because my parents got divorced when I was young. My mother left and I didn't see her for years. I want to be able to tell Jack what he was like when he was a baby. Now I'm supposed to go back to work, but if I'm not here with him, I think I'll feel like a bad mother."

It is only natural to want to be a "good mother." We have found, however, that those who grew up in families where there was alcoholism, depression, an early loss from death or divorce, or some form of abuse, seem prone to thinking that there are either "good mothers" or "bad mothers." In their desire to repair past hurts and to be the "good mother," they often strive to be the opposite of their own mothers. This kind of thinking can trap women into making decisions that may not actually work for them. In doing so, these women set impossible expectations for themselves which ensure either daily falls from grace or years of sacrifice and resentment.

If these points strike a chord in you, or hit a nerve, take some time to evaluate how much the mission to repair childhood hurts is driving your thinking about work. And go easy on yourself. Working full-time doesn't mean that you are abandoning your baby. And being a full-time mother doesn't mean that you must sacrifice everything to your baby.

∽ CHILD CARE

Returning to work full-time is both a logistical challenge and an emotional one. All of the women we have met in our groups who have had to leave their baby in someone else's care to return to work full-time have experienced a sense of loss. If you or your partner cannot stay at home, or cannot share in the care of your baby, it will help you to find a caregiver whom you trust, like, and think will provide the same kind of high quality, caring interaction with your baby that you do.

"I got a call this morning from a nanny but I wasn't ready to talk to her," says Maggie. "I'm thinking, 'What do I ask her?' and she's saying, 'Can we set up an interview?' So I said, 'I can't find my datebook.' "

"I don't want to have to look for child care," says Leslie. "How can I find someone I know I can trust and feel confident about when I'm still learning what it's like to be a parent myself?"

You may be going back to work in a month and still be unable to set up interviews with potential caregivers or to establish a working relationship with one. It may seem frightening or even unthinkable to hire someone to take care of your infant child. A new mother may wonder if anyone could possibly be as attentive to her infant as she is. It helps to start talking with child care professionals to get past these initial fears. For most women considering child care, the anticipation is far worse than the reality.

"I had a strong reaction against the first few people I interviewed," says Alicia. "But I probably didn't want to like anyone. I wasn't very objective about the whole thing but I told myself I was going to trust my gut. I think that's actually a pretty safe rule in this case. Because it was also my gut that liked Mary. It wasn't anything she said, it just felt right. I think you'll know it when it's right. Mary is gentle and nurturing. Her references were excellent. My husband and I felt she was just the right person for Keith and for us. And so far she is working out well. She has her opinions, but that's good. She never makes me feel like she's taking over, which for me is key."

Fears and lack of information can delay a decision to hire a caregiver, can leave you stranded without help for the wrong reasons. It's important, however, to differentiate between anxiety about finding the right caregiver and an inner voice trying to make itself heard. If you have committed yourself to return to work and truly don't want to, you may resist child care as a sort of unconscious subterfuge as you stall for time, trying to change your mind.

"I have a sitter once a week right now, just to get acquainted and break her in," says Nan. "It has been torture working out a relationship with her because I'm torn about it. I take all my anxieties out on her. I follow her around the house making sure she does everything exactly like I do with the baby."

It takes time to let yourself rely on your baby-sitter, and to let go of the controls for a while. One of the reasons you may not want to let go is that you fear your baby will become more attached to the baby-sitter than to you. Many new mothers who are returning to work worry about this. While you are still new to your role, your caretaker may be skillful and confident. You want someone who will come to care deeply for your child, but you're not sure how you feel about your child caring deeply for her. As you picture another woman spending nine hours a day, five days a week with your baby, you wonder, how could she *not* become more important than me?

Babies keep their strong attachments to their working mothers. While a consistent caregiver may become a beloved person in your child's life, she will not usurp your primary role. It is inevitable though, that working mothers experience some sense of jealousy and competition with their child's nanny, baby-sitter, or day-care professional. If, however, your feelings are preoccupying or persistent, your reasons are worth exploring. Are you resentful about going back to work? Does your child's day-care center not meet your standards? Or, is your child's caregiver provoking you by an attitude of possessiveness or authority about your child?

"My homecomings at the end of the day had always been a wonderful time with Keith," says Alicia. "I would get very excited to see him on my commute and when I got out of the subway I'd practically be running up the block. When I came in the door his eyes would light up and he would be all smiles and I would swoop him into my arms and cover him with kisses and tell him how much I missed him.

"But when he was about four months old that changed. When I came through the door he wouldn't look at me. Sometimes he would cry. I think he was mad at me. It felt like he was saying, 'I like Mary better. Go away!' It broke my heart."

Keith's reaction to his mother's homecomings is painful for her but it can be looked at in a different, more positive way. Keith is attached primarily to his mother, Alicia, but also to Mary, his nanny. When Alicia leaves in the morning Keith misses her and has to muster up resources to be without her. During the day Keith plays and eats and sleeps well and is affectionate and happy with Mary. But, upon Alicia's return he is reminded of how much he has missed her. Like most babies and young children he has saved up his feelings for his mother. By shunning Alicia or crying when she comes home, he is confirming (albeit in an upsetting way) that she *is* his most important person.

Fortunately, Mary has a lot of experience with babies and is sensitive to Alicia's feelings. She and Alicia talked about the change in Keith's response. Mary suggested a gradual warm-up period upon Alicia's return home to allow Keith time to make the transition on his terms.

"And it worked," Alicia says. "If I was quiet and casual about my return home, in a few minutes Keith would reach for me in his old, affectionate, loving way."

It is important to let your child's caregiver relieve you of your responsibilities. But it is equally important to establish a good rapport with her, to exchange opinions and to talk each day about what your child did. If your child is at a day-care center, you can spend some time with him there. Your active involvement will help you feel included in your baby's day, will keep you informed of the style of care given and give you the opportunity to discuss your baby's development.

Babies are capable of expanding their world to include additional surrogate nurturers and still keep their primary attachment to their mothers. The daily changing of hands from mother to caregiver can become part of your baby's routine in a positive way. One more person who loves him and is interested in building his confidence, in providing stimulation and comfort will enrich him.

∽ YOU, YOUR HUSBAND, AND WORK

Your husband's response to parenting, his self-image as a provider for his family, his feelings about you as a mother and the amount of child care and household responsibilities he is willing and able to take on will greatly influence your decision about work. Fatherhood can bring out some wonderful and some not-so-wonderful sides to your husband which you may never have seen before. His behavior may confuse you at times, fill you with pride and love one minute and with anger the next. Like you, your husband is beginnning a new phase in life. He may not be adapting to all the changes at home as well as he lets on. A new father may have a heightened, and sometimes burdensome, sense of responsibility for the family's financial security. He may feel pressured to live up to society's standards as the "head of the family." Men and women alike report how helpful it is to talk openly about the changes that are taking place. Whether or not you are returning to your job, the amount of support you have from your husband, how involved he is personally in the care of your baby and how well you work together as a couple will make a crucial difference to your experience of parenting.

Over the years we have known a significant number of new fathers who have decided to be integrally involved in the raising of their children. In these families, the couples have worked out diverse and creative plans of cooperative schedules. Examples of couples we've known include one in which the new mother worked three-quarter-time outside the home as a doctor, while the new father stayed home as the primary caretaker, pursuing his artistic career part-time; another in which the mother worked half-time as an architect and the father worked half-time as a musical producer, each sharing in the daytime care of their baby; another in which the mother worked outside of the home in the mornings at a family-owned business and the father worked outside the home in the afternoons and evenings.

These kinds of arrangements usually entail a sacrifice in income and often women feel more pressure themselves to bring in the paycheck. Some even find that they resent their husbands for not taking the more traditional role of breadwinner and envy them their time with the baby. But more commonly in those families in which the men have taken on central parenting roles, the women have found that their decisions about going back to work are less conflicted, less full of guilt. They feel that leaving the baby with his father is a plus for the whole family. Most of these women report a great satisfaction at sharing the responsibility of their new baby's needs with their husbands.

Nan and Rick

Nan's story is a classic one of push and pull. She loves her baby. She loves her husband. She loves her work. And yet they each pull her in different directions. A successful photo stylist, Nan worked for six years in her field and had made a name for herself. As she describes it, her career made up ninety percent of her life. Both she and her husband, Rick, a commercial photographer, are ambitious and driven. They agree that one secret to their good relationship is their shared interest in each other's professional endeavors. Then came Emma.

"Emma was a surprise," Nan confesses. "Let's just say she was not on my list. Rick and I were thinking we'd have a baby one day. But not for a few years. Neither one of us was ready for this. After my mother died I dove into my career. It's a very high-paced lifestyle, lots of travel, lots of sixteen-hour days. I've loved it, but it's not the kind of job you can do when you have a baby.

"I arranged for a three-month maternity leave, but the longer I'm away from my job the more I realize I can't do my career and be a mother. The other night my husband said, 'You can do it. You can do it. You've always been able to do everything. You can do both.' I wanted to say 'yes,' too, so I was nodding, but I felt sick until finally I said, 'Wait a minute! I don't think I can do both.' That was a breakthrough for me.

"Right now I'm helping a friend from work on one small assignment. I do some telephone work during Emma's naps. It's amazing how much more efficient I am now. It's tempting to think I could do regular freelance work. But even now when Emma wakes up and I'm in the middle of something I feel like screaming. It's hard to shift gears. I'm not sure how I'm going to work this all out. But I know I want to be home more than I thought I would. Rick thinks I can do more freelance work, but even this tiny juggling act feels crazed.

"At first Rick said he thought I would be unhappy if I gave up my career altogether. Then we got more to the heart of it. His mother had been self-sacrificing and miserable and Rick was afraid I would turn into that type of mother if I didn't keep my career going full steam. Between Rick's pressure and my own, I started to think I *should* be able to do it all," says Nan. "But how can I take care of Emma, keep the house going, and do freelance work at the same time?"

A woman's decision about work is often tailored by her husband's needs, fears, or desires. But it would be impossible for Nan "to do it all," as Rick had suggested. Regardless of a couple's political or emotional commitment to equality between the sexes, when a baby comes into the picture, the division of labor between a husband and wife typically becomes more conventional. As new parents, both men and women tend to slip into old roles from their childhood regarding who does what at home. Often men think they are not responsible for the housework. Simultaneously, women think themselves to be ultimately responsible for all the housework and all the baby care. It takes time to work out new roles and ways of managing the additional tasks. The division of labor in the house is a critical factor in your decision about work. A husband who supports your decision in both thought and action can make the key difference to making life feel manageable.

It can be helpful for you as a couple to sit down together and define the hundreds of chores required to keep your household and family up and running. Include all baby care activities such as bathing, changing, feeding, and bedtime; all household duties such as laundry, bed-making, grocery shopping, cooking, and cleaning, plus all inside and outside chores related to your home like taking out the garbage, taking care of the lawn, repairing faucets, and cleaning windows; all money-earning activities, work outside the home, accounting and paperwork duties; and all tasks associated with social activities, like buying gifts, sending cards, making telephone calls, and helping family members and friends.

As you talk about all of these tasks, decide together who will do them, how and when they will be taken care of, if they have to be done at all, and how much outside household or child care help you need and can afford. Some women in our groups tell us that their husbands would not consider doing this exercise, that it would be a no-win battle better avoided. But even if your husband is set in his ways, traditional in his views, or overworked himself, do not underestimate him. Also, no matter what he can or cannot do to help, it is important for him to be aware of the labor-intensive demands of motherhood. Writing this kind of a list will make the invisible work become visible. It can show both husband and wife the amount of time and effort it takes for a family simply to manage. If you and your husband can share the responsibilities, the load will be lightened, both physically and psychologically and, most important, you will feel more like partners.

∽ TRYING TO DO IT ALL

In an attempt to bridge two worlds, women may fantasize about being full-time mothers *and* working on their careers. Nan had an image of herself working at her drafting table, her baby happily playing with blocks at her feet. Elizabeth had a vision of writing during Lucy's naps. Maggie had an idea that she would take her baby to work with her. All mothers-to-be daydream about life with their babies, but few envision the consuming nature of full-time motherhood.

Some of the mothers in our groups have become so conflicted at the thought of leaving their babies to return to work, they begin a vicious routine of trying to do two jobs without any help. They delude themselves into thinking that with extra effort this might be possible and even reasonable. As a long-term solution, it is not. No matter how much you may want to fill both roles, it is not realistic to consider this as an option. Realizing that you cannot do it all is crucial to your well-being.

∽ MONEY

"Everyone is talking about how hard it is to make a decision about work," Maggie blurts out. "Doesn't it all come down to money? A paycheck? Your budget?"

Even though life at home has been a big adjustment, Maggie is upset at the prospect of returning to work and is trying to figure out some way to change her plans. Meanwhile, money is tight and her husband wants her to return to work.

Marta has returned to her job as a social worker. As a single parent, financial pressures dictate her decisions. "I really don't have a choice. I'm the only breadwinner. I have to work. Maybe that makes it easier," she says.

For most, money *is* the key factor in the decision about work. A baby brings new, immediate expenses as well as new, long-range financial goals.

Marta has no option but to work. Alicia is committed to her career. But it is for those who are wavering, like Maggie, Elizabeth, and Leslie, that money can become a source of personal anxiety or marital conflict. Debits and assets may seem to add up in neat columns, but the issue of money is an elusive, evocative, and emotionally charged one. It is often the major obstacle, real or symbolic, to making the best decision for you about your work life.

∽ THE VALUE OF YOUR WORK AS MOTHER

The work world does not recognize, allow for, or give credit to motherhood. The longer you are out of the workforce, the harder it is to get back in and the less you may command in salary. After even a few years of projects, paychecks, and promotions, the transition to nonsalaried motherhood is difficult. As a result, even mothers tend to undervalue their role. It is especially important for both you and your husband to give credit, value, and respect to the job of mother. A few of the mothers in our group do. Alicia says, "My job at the office is a piece of cake compared to the job of mothering." Ronnie, reflecting on her days as a teacher, adds, "It's easier to take care of twenty-five second graders than one baby."

It may make you uneasy to discuss money and motherhood in the same breath. In truth, it would be impossible to put a price tag on nurturing or love. But it is important to take an honest look at what making money means to you, and what *not* making money means to you.

"Each time my husband and I say we should sit down and figure out how our finances work, and whether or not I have to go back to work, my mind goes blank," says Leslie. "I say I'll think about it tomorrow, but I never do."

It is understandable that Leslie is having difficulty grappling with the myriad implications of the financial situation of her family. It may be especially threatening for her to consider what it means not to be making money herself. Making money is tied up with self-esteem, independence, power, control, and prestige. Between a husband and wife, money is part of an intricate system of checks and balances. No matter how much money you earn or need, financial issues pack an emotional wallop. Your decision about work is also about what you are willing to sacrifice and what you are not. It is about priorities and about the values you attach to them.

Unless your parents were the exception to the rule, you probably grew up in a family in which your mother was financially dependent on your father. Now a mother yourself, you may begin to feel insecure about money if you are not bringing in a paycheck; you may feel dependent on your husband, no longer his equal. Many women who are full-time mothers fall into the habit of asking their husbands for money as if it were an allowance. They feel guilty when they spend money, even when it is on household necessities, and find it increasingly difficult to spend money on themselves.

It can be an important part of adjusting to new parenthood to talk with your husband about money and to participate in your family's finances. Many couples use seemingly logical methods to determine whether or not a mother should go back to work. Often they look only to see whether the woman's salary will cover the costs of day care or a baby-sitter. This is a biased method of accounting which assumes that the woman's work must cover the child's care. It also excludes such options as cutting back, sharing baby care, or of borrowing money for a limited period of time. And it discourages the idea of part-time work, which is often the most appealing solution. Child care costs should be a joint financial responsibility and should come out of the family pot, not solely from the woman's earnings. If, for the time being, you are a one-paycheck family, try to see your partner's salary as the *family* income. Both you and your husband are doing work vital to your family.

∾ PUSH THE SYSTEM

"The work world isn't mother-friendly," says Leslie.

While the current generation of mothers has entered the workforce in record numbers, this country's workplaces are not accommodating to their personal needs. Women who push the system are slowly effecting change. Work/family arrangements *are* becoming more common today in American business. Many of the bigger companies offer options such as job sharing, telecommuting, and on-site day care.

When options are limited, creative solutions are often the best answer. Push the system to see whether you can create a new arrangement that suits your needs. Treat your idea as you might a business proposal. Go directly to the top and approach the person who makes these decisions with an offer that will intrigue him or her. Women who are hesitant to ask for a more flexible work schedule assume an exception won't be made on the basis of their status as a new mother. Yet we do hear stories of success, or at least of partial success, when women do not accept the status quo.

Some employers are open to longer maternity leaves with partial pay. Some companies offer options to maternity leaves such as unpaid extensions. Some women "save up" their vacation days and lump these together with their maternity leave to stretch out their time at home with their new baby. It is a good idea to request as much leave time as you can possibly get. It is almost always easier to go back to work earlier than expected than it is to extend a maternity leave. Some professions, teaching for example, are amenable to full year leaves of absence. Some businesses and many state and federal workplaces offer affordable, flexible, on-site day care. Today over half of all mothers with infant children are working. The structure of American business has the potential to be much more in tune with the needs of working mothers and is gradually being shaped in that direction. The Family and Medical Leave Act of 1993 requires employers of fifty or more workers to provide their employees with up to twelve weeks of unpaid leave for sickness in the family or for the birth or adoption of a baby. A father as well as a mother can now take family leave during his wife's childbirth and recovery. America has finally joined the ranks of some seventy-two countries worldwide that provide protected family and medical leave policies for working parents.

～ STRIVING FOR BALANCE

"With Lucy at day care a few times a week I think she gets a better mother out of the deal," says Elizabeth. "After I've had time to do my work I feel more balanced. Then I can spend time with Lucy without any misgivings."

Everyone's "balance" will be different. From the outside, it may appear that Alicia is back full tilt at her job. But her priorities have shifted. She no longer travels for her company because she wants to be with her baby part of every day. And she takes a day off from work every two or three weeks. Home with her baby full-time, Jane's new balance entailed learning that she had to take time for herself. Jane's mother has filled the role of trusted baby-sitter with great ease and pleasure. Elizabeth's new balance will eventually include a more equal sharing of Lucy's care with her husband. And over time Elizabeth plans to assume more and more of the breadwinning responsibilities as Jonathan takes on more of the care of their baby. Ronnie's new balance came in stages. She left her elementary school teaching job to be home full-time with her baby. She made friends with a number of other new mothers and also kept in touch with her colleagues. She saw a need for quality day care in her neighborhood and began to formulate an idea that could one day accommodate mothering and a work life related to her expertise—running a family day care herself.

Your balance will keep changing with time. You will need to reassess your feelings and decisions as you and your family grow. Your husband's role also plays an important part. New phases of development in your child will elicit new emotions from you. Motherhood is a time to grow and learn about yourself and your life goals. It is a time of joy and playfulness. It is a time of increased responsibilities. It is in everyone's best interests—yours, your husband's, your baby's, your boss's—to figure out what you can do and what you want to do. There may not be a single "right" choice, but there is one that is manageable and balanced for you.

THREE

Feeding and Nurturing
Trusting Your Baby's Appetite

Feeding a baby is part of the very earliest communication between parent and child. More than simply a matter of providing nutrition, the process triggers a pattern of responses in both infant and parent. Each time you respond to your baby's signal of hunger by offering milk you are reinforcing her ability to communicate hunger. Each time you stop feeding your baby when she indicates that she is no longer hungry, you are respecting her ability to express that. Your reading of, and response to, your baby's cues helps to teach her to understand her own feelings of hunger and fullness as it strengthens her sense of trust in herself, in you, and in the world around her. And with each feeding that goes well, your sense of confidence as a nurturer will build.

"When Justin is at my breast I think we are both truly blissful," says Jane. "But the whole process of breast feeding hasn't been easy."

Jane's belief in, commitment to, and emotional satisfaction from breast feeding carried her through two challenging months with her baby. Justin's birth weight of six pounds, two ounces, was on the low end of average. He was wiry, active, and hungry, needing to nurse around the clock, every one to two hours.

"I knew I wanted to breast-feed, but I never anticipated what it would entail. It was as if he couldn't get enough," Jane explains. "Life was one extended feeding, day and night. I had never been so tired. And I began to wonder if I was producing enough milk. But my mother told me that as a baby I had gained weight very slowly, too. And I was a formula baby, but she said I was always hungry, too.

"When Justin was four weeks my left nipple cracked. I could only nurse on the right side and then my left breast became engorged. I remember thinking—'Great, what next?' Well next came a breast infection. I had a fever for two days. The whole thing was a nightmare.

"My mother was over every day. And Ethan got off from work early every afternoon for a week to help out. I couldn't do anything. I needed hot and cold compresses on my breasts. And sleep. It was the most I could do to wake up to nurse Justin."

"The pediatrician thought Justin wasn't getting enough milk from me and recommended that I supplement with formula. I balked. I know there isn't anything wrong with formula, but it wasn't what I wanted to do."

Justin's doctor agreed to support Jane's decision to continue solely with breast feeding only if Jane agreed to bring Justin in every week to have his weight gain monitored. Antibiotics cleared up Jane's breast infection quickly, and she was able to nurse comfortably again within a few days.

"I'm really glad we stuck it out," Jane finishes. "Justin's appetite has become less voracious. He's on a more regular nursing schedule now. He's still on the low end of the charts. But he's gaining weight and thriving."

⌒ BREAST FEEDING OR BOTTLE FEEDING

The decision to breast- or bottle-feed your baby is an intensely personal one. Whether you are nursing or giving your baby formula from a bottle, there are benefits to each choice.

Breast milk is more easily digested by babies, contains important antibodies that supplement the baby's developing immune system, and presents less risk of allergy. It satisfies a baby's thirst, hunger, and sucking needs. Breast feeding is also good for the mother. Women who breastfeed have a reduced incidence of breast cancer. Additionally, hormones associated with breast feeding help return the mother's uterus to its original size more quickly. Nursing burns calories and helps some new mothers to lose weight. Breast milk is convenient, portable, and cost-free.

Formula can keep a baby satisfied longer and some mothers say it helps their babies to sleep for longer stretches at a time. Unlike breast milk, formula can be measured and a baby's daily intake gauged. Bottle feeding allows a mother certain freedoms—to feed her baby while on line at the supermarket, for example; to eat spicy foods, drink alcohol, or take medicines that might otherwise be restricted from a nursing mother's diet. There is less physical strain on her body. Fathers and other family members can be more involved with this part of child care and middle-of-the-night feedings can be shared.

When it is possible and pleasurable for a woman to do so, we advocate breast feeding. Even a week of breast feeding is worthwhile, giving the baby colustrum and you the chance to try nursing. And it is not a failure to stop. More important than the way a baby is fed, however, is that a mother and her baby are comfortable and happy together. Both breast and bottle feeding provide the nutrition a baby needs. Both offer the chance for genuine intimacy and attachment between a mother and her baby.

Breast Feeding—The Highs and Lows

Though breast feeding can come to feel easy and comfortable for both mother and baby, it is important to realize that it can be, and often is, difficult. This is especially true during the beginning weeks. Breast feeding is not a completely instinctive act for the mother. Sometimes it does not come easily to the infant either. Once a mother and baby have mastered the fine art of nursing, many describe it as a deeply satisfying experience. Ronnie describes a state of "nursing nirvana" which she slips into while breast feeding Elyse, a sense of newfound purpose and well-being. Most mothers will agree that when nursing is going well, they feel confident, proud, and relaxed.

"What's the opposite of nursing nirvana?" Nan asks. "When Emma latches on to my breast, it's a form of torture! And what happens when they get teeth?"

It requires a certain amount of confidence to proceed in the face of sore nipples, a demanding feeding schedule, or feelings of frustration and exhaustion. If you do run into difficulties and are without support, you may experience some loneliness, even some desperation. You may be feeling inadequate and insecure. When you seek out help, it may seem there are only two camps of thinking: those ardently in favor of breast feeding and those who simply say 'Use formula.' Both seem to focus on the end and not the process and can disregard a mother's feelings. Sometimes all it takes for a new mother to get on track is some encouragement and advice. But sometimes, for one reason or another, breast feeding doesn't work out. Some babies develop lactose intolerance or milk allergies. Others do not gain weight well.

If there are no medical reasons against it, and you want to breast-feed but are having some trouble with it, we recommend that you give yourself at least a month before you decide to change course. Talk with your pediatrician and stay in regular touch with him or her throughout this early period. Enlist the support of an experienced friend or the professional assistance of a lactation specialist. An experienced mother is often the most helpful and her practiced eye may see that you are holding your baby in an awkward position or that you are not drinking as much water as you should be. Sometimes the company and support of a friend will relax you enough to make nursing less stressful. Once mothers get through the initial, trying weeks, most agree breast feeding is well worth the effort.

Changing Theories

For most of the twentieth century, and since the invention of formula, there has been great pressure on new mothers to bottle-feed their babies. Recently the pendulum has swung back the other way in favor of breast feeding. Of the nine mothers in the group, seven chose to breast-feed and two use formula. Alicia, a lawyer back at work full-time, found the pressure to breast-feed offensive.

"Six hours after Keith was born someone from the hospital came to my room and announced that she was there to help me with breast feeding," Alicia recounts. "She didn't ask me what I planned to do. According to her, breast feeding was the only way to go. When I told her I had decided to use formula she said I would be cheating myself and my baby if I didn't breast-feed and that plenty of working mothers nursed their babies. I felt like she was on a mission."

Many women report receiving inordinate pressure to nurse their babies—from health professionals, from the media, from other mothers. Some say they feel as if there was no choice. Alicia did not have a personal desire to breast-feed and the demands of her job made it an unrealistic goal. Fortunately she was confident in her decision.

Many women prefer to bottle-feed their babies. It is how they were fed and how their mothers fed their siblings, it is what they grew up accustomed to seeing, and it seems the most comfortable and natural choice to them now. In some instances a woman may not have a choice. Illness may prevent her from nursing, or her baby's illness may necessitate her being bottle-fed. If you find yourself in circumstances which do not favor breast feeding, or if you prefer to bottle-feed, you may feel some guilt from the pressures around you. Again, how you feed your baby is not what is ultimately important. Nurturing and closeness are.

At this, Marta, who looks as though she's been holding her breath, exhales.

"This whole topic is hard for me," she says. "But I promised myself I was going to talk about it. I'm not having practical difficulties with Sarah's feeding. It's really more my problem. Sarah's adopted, so I'm not going to be nursing, but I'm envious of all of you who can. I sometimes wonder—Does Sarah want to nurse? Does she know I'm *not* her birth mother? Will I ever really feel like her mother? It probably sounds crazy to you."

"I don't think it's crazy," Ronnie responds. "I'd feel the same way. I *am* nursing Elyse and even so I feel like a fake sometimes. In the beginning I kind of pretended to know what I was doing. I thought to myself, 'A real mother would instinctively know.' When I was in the hospital I wondered when the 'real mother' would come to take over."

Many of the adoptive mothers in our groups have reacted as Marta has, assuming that their insecurities are due to their adoptive status. It is helpful for Marta to hear other mothers talk about their own feelings of uncertainty or inadequacy. Whether you nurse or use formula, feeding a baby is not as simple or straightforward as it looks. It can be a highly emotional process. It helps to know that with time, ease and confidence will come.

∽ YOUR OWN EATING HISTORY

Food plays a powerful role in our lives. It is and always will be associated with deeply cherished rituals and celebrations. Tastes and aromas can unlock childhood memories. Food and eating give a rhythm to the days and mark the passage of seasons and holidays. Feelings about food, eating, and mealtimes from your own childhood will affect your response to feeding your baby.

In today's culture, dieting has become a way of life for many women. For them, food is a constant preoccupation, an emotional symbol, even an enemy. It is associated with self-image, anxiety, and denial. The high numbers of women with eating disorders in this country point to the connections between mental health and eating. As a mother embarking on the process of teaching another human being about food, it can be helpful and important to look at your own feelings about food, weight, and body image.

This strikes a chord for Elizabeth who says, "I think I do trust Lucy's appetite but every once in a while I look down at her as she's guzzling away and I think—'She's a little piglet!' She seems hungry all the time, and I worry that she's going to be fat.

"At her three-month checkup Lucy weighed fifteen pounds! Mostly I'm glad that she is a good eater, but there's a voice inside me that keeps saying, 'She's going to be a fat kid if you don't watch out.' "

Many new mothers worry about under- or overfeeding their babies. Monthly visits to the pediatrician that confirm an average and steady weight gain do little to help. Sometimes this worry is set off when a mother and baby have a difficult time getting started with breast feeding or when, for example, a baby has colic and seems to find relief only when she is eating. If a mother's preoccupations linger despite the fact that her baby is thriving, her own history may offer an explanation.

Elizabeth tells us that she never had a weight problem, but that her sister Patricia did, and that she was made fun of, especially by their brother.

"I don't know if Patricia suffered more from being chubby or from all the nasty comments she got," Elizabeth tells the group. "She was called 'Fatty Patty' most of her childhood. And my parents allowed that kind of name-calling to go on within the family.

"Lucy actually reminds me of my sister in some ways," Elizabeth muses. "Her eyes, her expressions, and certainly in her need to always have something in her mouth."

Elizabeth never had weight problems herself, but the message in her family was clear—fat was bad and cause for ridicule. For years Elizabeth harbored a certain guilt for being the thin one. But in her adult years, Patricia successfully shed her extra weight, and Elizabeth believed that childhood chapter to be closed. She sees, however, that many of her current feelings about food and weight stem from these early experiences and that this is getting tangled up with her attitudes about feeding Lucy.

Young girls get the message early in our society that there is an ideal body type—thin—which they must try to conform to, no matter how they came into the world. Strong feelings of guilt, revulsion, anxiety about control, desire for affection and worry about appearance can become associated with the wonderful act of eating. Food and drink have also taken on the roles of stimulants and relaxants. As a result, over time women have lost their trust in their natural appetites. It is no wonder, therefore, that some mothers do not trust their babies' appetites either. But they can. A healthy baby will naturally eat the amount she or he needs. Mothers offer a great gift to their children by giving them a sense of control over the eating process, as well as a natural, unencumbered appreciation for food.

ᥐ A DEVELOPMENTAL MODEL

In the womb a baby is fed by a continuous flow from her mother's bloodstream. She does not experience hunger or fullness. A baby is born with an innate sucking reflex, but she has to learn how her newly separate body works and to communicate when she is hungry and when she is full. A mother's job is to learn how to interpret her baby's signals, to respond and ultimately to help her baby feel satisfied and comfortable.

A newborn's first three months are generally a period of intense, focused feeding. Babies will close their eyes, work hard, and expend lots of energy as they nurse or bottle-feed. They finish sweaty and often tired. As you get to know your baby you will come to know how she likes to be held during a feeding, how long her feedings last, when and how she needs to be burped, and how long before she will feel hunger again. Once feeding is going smoothly, many mothers feel in tune with their babies, anticipating their hunger needs instinctively. Some nursing mothers describe waking in the middle of the night as their milk comes in, seconds *before* the baby awakens and cries. When a baby's hunger cries are answered, her hunger is replaced with a sense of well-being. These good feelings come to be associated with the breast or bottle and also with the mother—how she smells, feels, holds, speaks, and caresses while she feeds.

ᥐ HUNGER AND COMFORT

"I nurse Elyse every couple of hours," says Ronnie. "Sometimes she's hungry but sometimes she just needs to be comforted. My husband says, 'She's always nursing!' But if that's what she wants, why shouldn't I? Isn't that reasonable?''

If it is soothing and pleasant for both of you, then it is reasonable and appropriate in these early months to offer your baby your breast whenever she seems to want it. Suckling can often be as much for comfort, warmth, and closeness as it is for sustenance.

Both breast- and bottle-fed babies derive great comfort from sucking. But it can be hard to judge what a baby needs. Babies who are tired, overstimulated, or uncomfortable may behave as if they are hungry by crying, rooting at your breast, or making sucking sounds for a bottle. If you think it seems early for her to need to eat again, you can try something other than feeding to try to soothe her. Offer a pacifier, your finger, her fingers or thumb to suck on. If one of these satisfies your baby, she may calm easily or drift to sleep.

All babies are different. Each baby comes into the world with his own specific body type, energy level, caloric needs, and feeding style. Babies go through phases, appetite spurts, growth spurts, and slower periods. Even as it waxes and wanes, your baby's appetite is to be trusted.

Like Elizabeth's baby, Lucy, some babies can only be described as born eaters. They have an instinctive capacity to latch on to the nipple and to suck. Some "born eaters" have built-in timetables and develop an eating schedule early on. Others are not as predictable; they wake and feed irregularly and seem to take different amounts each time. Nan's baby, Emma, can be described as a grazer. She snacks on and off throughout the day, taking small amounts frequently. Ronnie's baby, Elyse, nurses well but regularly spits up afterward. Pediatricians reassure mothers that spitting-up is common and usually will pass by the first birthday. In the first weeks Jessica found that it helped if she loosely swaddled Nell for her feedings. Now Jessica finds that it helps when she nurses Nell in a dark, quiet room. Nell often also requires extra comforting after a feeding. Some babies are so sleepy during their first weeks of life that a feeding tires them out and they will fall asleep midway, more content to snooze than to eat. Some babies may have difficulty getting their mouth positioned on the nipple correctly and need help each time. Other babies resist the nestle-in-your-arms, rock-a-bye-baby position of feeding. All babies need physical contact, especially at mealtimes. Experiment with a variety of positions until you find one that is mutually comfortable for you and your child.

Babies vary in their feeding schedules. To underscore this point we asked Nan and Ronnie to compare Emma's and Elyse's schedules. Their babies were both born at full term, both are breast-feeding, weigh within a few ounces of each other, and are less than two weeks apart in age. Their feeding schedules, however, are very different.

Emma is eight and a half weeks old. She wakes for her first nursing sometime around 6:00 A.M. Generally she nurses again at 8:00 A.M. before her morning nap and then after her nap at 10:00 A.M., and then again at 11:30 A.M. Most days she will nurse every two hours until bedtime at 10:30 P.M. She usually wakes sometime between 2:00 and 3:00 A.M. for her middle-of-the-night feeding.

Elyse is ten and a half weeks old. For over a month now, she has been waking up in the morning around 7:00 A.M., nursing, and then taking her morning nap. Usually she wakes to feed again sometime before 11:00 A.M. Then she doesn't need to eat again until the afternoon and usually not before 3:00 P.M. She nurses at 7:00 P.M. and before bedtime, around 11:00 P.M., and once during the night.

Both of these schedules are typical for infants and illustrate how very different babies can be in their daily rhythms. We encourage mothers to adopt a flexible approach to feeding during the first three months and to freely respond to their babies' cries of hunger. Most babies can tolerate hunger only in small doses before they cry out. To make an infant wait until the clock says it's time to eat can be overwhelming and disorganizing for her. Gradually your baby will eat larger amounts less frequently. A baby's early random schedule will naturally develop into a more predictable pattern.

⟱ COMBINING NURSING WITH BOTTLES

Many new mothers will want to nurse their babies as well as feed them from bottles. For these mothers we recommend introducing a bottle at three weeks. Starting this early can avoid some resistance to the bottle. Some babies will easily switch back and forth between these two methods. Other babies are more finicky. Initially, breast-fed babies can be adamant about refusing a bottle. In this case, it might help to experiment with timing. Offer a bottle when your baby is in an easy, good mood. Try after he has nursed on one breast and taken the edge off of his hunger. Or, try first thing in the morning or during a middle-of-the-night feeding.

As important as the timing is your attitude about introducing a bottle. Offer your baby a bottle, but don't push it. Try to stay flexible and playful. After a few minutes of

play see this as a successful attempt and stop, even if she
has taken no milk. Try again later in the day. Most babies
will take to a bottle after a week or two of being offered
it in an easygoing manner. For those babies who repeat-
edly reject a bottle, some parents have reported that fast,
rhythmic rocking while offering a bottle can work. They
describe the rocking as hypnotic. And then, once the adjustment to the bottle has been made, the rocking is no
longer necessary.

The familiar smell of mother's milk can confuse and
frustrate a baby who is being offered a bottle for the first
time. For this reason many experts advise that a mother
stay out of this process altogether. But in many cases we
have found that the mother is precisely the best person
to take on this task. Her early weeks and months of caring
for her baby have taught her to understand her baby's
signals and nuances of behavior better than anyone else.
As a result she is usually in the best position to teach her
baby this new skill.

"I've got such mixed feelings about weaning," says
Nan. "I'm ready to reclaim my body, but I know that
breast milk is good for Emma. The thing is I'm considering taking on another freelance job and I have to think
about cutting down."

Breast feeding works on supply and demand. Less milk
is produced when less milk is taken. As long as you continue to breast-feed every morning, evening, and again
before you put your baby to bed at night, you should be
able to continue for as long as you like. Some women
take a breast pump to work. But if you want to breast-
feed at the beginning and end of the day, pumping may
not be necessary. As you nurse less frequently, your
breasts will begin to get smaller and you might feel as

though you have less milk. However, in most cases you *are* still producing enough milk to meet the demands of your baby's feeding schedule. And, if you change your mind and decide to breast-feed more often, you can make a gradual increase as well.

∽ YOUR BABY GREETS THE WORLD

"Do you see this?" Maggie asks, nodding toward Jack, who is at her breast.

"He's hungry. He starts to nurse. And then he pulls away from me. Sometimes he literally spits out my breast!"

Jack has, in fact, pulled off of Maggie's breast, is peeking out from under her oversize shirt and looking around the room.

"I *know* he's hungry," says Maggie. "He hasn't eaten in four hours."

Maggie holds Jack horizontally, tucks him back in under part of her shirt, and offers her breast again. But Jack refuses.

"This drives me crazy. I've heard about self-weaning, but I didn't think it could happen so soon. He may be ready, but I'm not!"

As a baby passes the three-month mark, her focus will widen to greet the world. Her time of frequent and focused feeding is drawing to an end. Instead of giving full attention to the breast or bottle, she can become distracted by the sights and sounds around her. During a feeding your baby may stop to look about. She can take in her surroundings with more sustained interested now. She might return to the breast or bottle for a few swallows and then pull off again to smile, to grab at your hair, or to bang on the bottle with her tiny fist.

Many nursing mothers misinterpret these changes as the first indications of a natural self-weaning. It *can* look and feel as if your baby is rejecting your breast and it's not surprising that a new mother might think this. The resulting stop and start process of feeding will take longer and may frustrate you but it does not mean your baby has lost interest in nursing. There is simply more competition for her attention as she discovers the world around her. During this new halting phase of feeding, it's important to let your baby explore, turn, push away, and then return for more, both of you participating in the give-and-take of feeding and socializing. Remember that the buttons on your blouse are wonderfully compelling to a baby. By allowing for some play and socializing, you foster her sense of enjoyment during feedings. You may find that the early morning and bedtime feedings retain the focused quality of the earlier months. But don't expect your four-month-old to nurse continuously while three people are talking in the room. Those people, your conversation and gestures are newly fascinating to her.

"Sometimes I wish Lucy *would* let go of my breast!" says Elizabeth. "Especially before she looks around. But she holds on for dear life. At this point my breasts could probably stretch across the room!"

Maggie laughs along with the others but then becomes serious. She says with concern that Jack pulls off her breast all the time. "I can accept that he needs to look around, but I'm worried that he is not getting enough milk. He's not nursing as long as he used to."

By this age, your baby has become a stronger, more efficient sucker and can get what she needs in five to ten minutes at each breast rather than fifteen or twenty. You too have become more adept.

"This should all be reassuring to me," says Maggie. "But still this whole feeding thing makes me nervous. I feel myself almost getting angry when Jack pulls away."

It can be upsetting to acknowledge angry feelings toward your baby. At times like these of developmental change, feelings of confusion, frustration, and even anger are natural. They exist for all parents. Like loving feelings, they are part of the parent-child relationship. Usually, a little patience and the awareness of this natural developmental change can help. But for some new mothers, this transition is accompanied by ongoing worry, sadness, or anger. When these feelings persist, the mutual pleasure of the feeding experience can be undermined.

Until recently breast feeding was something Maggie truly enjoyed. In fact, she says it was one of her favorite parts of motherhood. But now the smooth flow between her and Jack has been disrupted. At first, she thought it was because she was nervous about the prospect of returning to work. But the anger and near-dread she now feels at each feeding indicate that Jack's behavior is stirring up other emotions in her.

When we ask Maggie why she thinks she's upset, she says self-mockingly, "I guess I never realized how important it is for me to feed people. Now I know why I'm in the restaurant business. When it comes down to it, I'm a real Jewish mother."

"Was your mother a 'real Jewish mother' too?" Marta asks Maggie.

"I guess so," Maggie replies. "She was a great cook. The kitchen was a wonderful place to be with her. She used to cook enough to feed any friends we brought home."

At this, Maggie's voice trails off and she bites her lip to keep herself from crying. During our discussion the previous week, Maggie had told us that her parents were divorced when she was eleven and that her mother had left home. Despite Maggie's recently renewed relationship with her mother and her loving attachment to her stepmother, Maggie is still sad and unresolved about her early loss. It's not uncommon that the issue of feeding will spark the fire of feelings from childhood. For Maggie, the loss of her mother set a sense of yearning in place. Twenty years later, as Maggie became a mother herself, these emotions are becoming vivid again.

During the first months of motherhood, breast feeding was a mutually nurturing experience for Maggie and her baby. But when Jack began the natural process of greeting the outside world, Maggie interpreted this as if he were rejecting her, as if he were leaving her; she felt that she had failed to keep him interested and close. Becoming a mother and having the support of this circle of mothers is helping Maggie to confront her past, to work to understand it better and to grow and change along with her baby. She must now grant Jack the right to be more independent without taking it personally. It will be the first such letting-go of many.

"I know I'll always be sad about my mother," Maggie says. "But I thought I had worked out most of those feelings and accepted them. I never expected to be loading them onto my own child!"

The experience of having a baby is one that sends women into realms left unattended for years, back to childhood scenes thought resolved, or at least safely

tucked away. Inevitably, the process of caring for and nurturing a baby will bring to the surface many old emotions.
This is part of the pain and richness that is parenthood.

～ WEANING

The decision about when to wean a baby from breast feeding is a highly personal one. No one's opinion is more
important than yours. If you decide to wean before your
baby's first birthday, however, we recommend weaning
to a bottle. Through the first twelve months a baby needs
the comfort that sucking provides. She also needs to be
held during feedings. The second half of the first year is
a time of dramatic motor development as well as one of
ambivalence about separations. Taking a bottle while
being held provides your baby with important security,
warmth, and confidence.

"I never imagined that feeding a baby could be so emotional," says Ronnie. "I feel like crying just thinking about
weaning Elyse. I know I'm going to have a hard time
with it, even when it is the right time."

Jane agrees. "I know what you mean. Now that things
have smoothed out with nursing I never want to stop."

"For me it will be something of a relief," says Nan.
"The truth is I'm looking forward to being done with
nursing."

When a mother weans her baby she may experience a
sense of liberation. She may celebrate her baby's growing
independence. Or this can be a time of sadness as she lets
go of her baby's infant stage. Weaning marks the end of a
primitive, physical, and psychological connection between
mother and child. A mild form of mourning at this stage

is not abnormal. Before long, however, new ways to communicate this bond with her baby will emerge.

Babies may regress temporarily or become especially needy when they are being weaned. Babies who are already using their fingers or a spoon to eat solid foods may go through a period during weaning in which they resist feeding themselves. In this case, indulge your baby for a few days. She will soon return to her more independent self.

"I can't imagine being able to soothe Elyse without nursing her," says Ronnie.

If nursing has been a primary way to comfort your baby when she is cranky, hurt, or frustrated, you may initially feel a little lost without it. Your baby may need extra cuddling, holding, and rocking to compensate for a while. Over time you will develop new ways to comfort your baby that work just as well as nursing once did.

Your baby may or may not express upset at being weaned. No matter what her reaction, use words to tell her what is happening. Try to be straightforward about it. And be careful not to place too much emphasis on the idea that your baby is a "big girl" or a "big boy" now. She is still very young and needs the comfort and closeness of mother.

✧ FEEDING AND INDEPENDENCE

As your baby grows, her sense of autonomy begins to blossom and she can take pride in feeding herself. Pediatricians vary in their opinions on this but generally agree that solid foods can be introduced anytime between four to six months.

Initially, your baby's eating experience is just that—an experience. She might swallow a little but mostly she will want to touch, squeeze, paint with, and drop food. Once the novelty has worn off and a degree of familiarity with new tastes and textures has been developed, a baby will generally turn her attention to actually eating. As important as offering food when you think your baby is hungry is allowing her to tell you when she is finished, whether it is after two tablespoons or a bowlful of cereal. Try not to cajole your baby into opening her mouth for one more bite because you want the bowl to be clean. Let your baby tell *you* when the meal is over. A baby has some very direct ways of saying this. One is to shut her mouth tightly. Another is to turn her head to the side. Another is to spit her food out. Although this seems pretty obvious, it is hard to know whether she is communicating "No more, thank you" or "I want to play for a minute." One workable rule of thumb is to offer a spoonful twice after the first rejection. If your baby's answer is "no" two more times, end the feeding.

Throughout a baby's first year, eating solids and making a mess are synonymous. A baby will taste, smell, rub, spit, dribble, and smear food everywhere. Her eyes remain completely innocent as she gives herself an oatmeal facial or a carrot shampoo. It may be easier to see the humor in this if you keep in mind that this will not last forever. Most mothers agree, however, that day in and day out, the mess a baby makes with food requires patience, tolerance, and plenty of cleaning up.

"The word 'mess' doesn't describe it," Leslie protests. "When it dries, that cereal is like papier-mâché. It gets everywhere. In his eyelashes and hair! I've always known

I was a clean-freak, but I never knew how bad it was before this."

There is no way to stop a baby from getting messy while learning to eat solid foods. Remember, a primary goal is for your baby to get a sense that eating is fun, that mealtimes are interesting, positive, and enjoyable, that she can explore a little bit and control a little bit. Your baby may want to eat and then baby-talk and laugh with you, or rub her hands in the food. She is in the process of learning a whole new way of eating.

It is not imperative that your baby eat the same amount at every meal. Like adults, babies can be more hungry or less hungry on different days. Don't worry if there are days when your baby won't eat much at all. All babies have appetite and growth spurts as well as lulls throughout this period.

As your baby grows, her desire for independence will increase but not uniformly in all areas of development. Her increase in autonomy regarding feeding may happen at six or seven months or not until the end or even beyond the first year. When it does happen, her opinions will become noticeably stronger and she will want to try to do things without your help. She may want to hold her spoon herself or she may want to scoop up her cereal with her hands. She may reject foods she had been eating with pleasure and show curiosity about new ones.

When your baby begins to show interest in feeding herself, you may not be able to tell the difference between eating and creative play. To allow for your baby's independent efforts *and* also get her fed, try using two spoons—one for her to play with and one for you to feed her with. Encourage your baby to feed herself and to try new things but allow her to develop at her own rate.

Some days she will feel less ambitious than others and will want you to feed her. Once a baby has learned to crawl and even more when she has learned to walk, it is very difficult for her to sit still in a high chair. Some parents have found that their baby will eat more and better if allowed to take breaks to crawl or walk around and then come back for more.

Some babies by nature are simply more finicky about food. This can be frustrating, but it is important to recognize and accept. If your baby wants only to eat four or five different foods and rejects all others, supply what she likes. Eating should not be an arena for confrontation. If you give her the message that what she likes is alright with you, you will sidestep battles about food that might otherwise last for years. Continue to introduce and offer new foods and encourage new tastes, but don't force the issue. Her tastes may broaden naturally with time.

"My memory doesn't go back to when I was a baby but I do remember my mother forcing me to eat vegetables when I was a kid. She was very strict about it. To this day I hate vegetables. I can't even look at some of them," says Jessica.

"My sister has two children," Jessica continues. "One is three years old and the other is eight months. My sister has given up trying to feed them a varied or balanced diet. She says they eat the same things over and over."

"I was a fussy eater too," says Ronnie. "For years I ate only foods that were white—cereal, toast, pasta. You wouldn't know it today. I eat everything now."

People usually think of a balanced diet in terms of a single meal. With babies and young children eating habits are so erratic that this balance usually occurs only over the course of a week or even up to a month. If your baby only wants to eat applesauce and cereal for three days in a row, and then switches to carrots and Cheerios for two days and then will only eat yogurt and macaroni for the next two, any given day seems unbalanced. But judged as a whole, over a longer period of weeks, her intake has been fairly well balanced. Looking to the future, about one-third of babies one to three years old will eat almost no vegetables whatsoever. And they survive. Vitamins abound in a variety of foods today, including formula, bread, and cereals.

⁓ FOLLOW YOUR BABY'S LEAD

One of the simplest and perhaps most important ideas to keep in mind regarding your baby's eating habits is that when they are offered food, babies and children will eat if they are hungry. They will not suppress hunger or withhold food from themselves. You can trust your baby's appetite. You can safely follow your baby's lead in this regard. A baby's sense of participation, control, and enjoyment in the eating process is paramount. It is the foundation of a child's healthy attitude toward eating and food. Your sense of enjoyment will be enhanced by hers.

The session is drawing to a close. As the women begin to gather their things and zip up their bags, Leslie approaches us and speaks quietly.

"This talk has been a huge relief for me," she says. "Ever since I got pregnant, I've been worried that somehow my own anxieties about eating would interfere with feeding my baby. I struggled for years with an eating disorder. I'm better now, but I still don't trust my instincts. The idea of trusting a baby's appetite makes it feel so much simpler. Who knows, maybe feeding Eric will end up helping me."

Our discussions on feeding are always full of practical concerns and nuts-and-bolts questions. But we have found that this subject can also motivate mothers to look inward, to consider their own personal histories and attitudes about food. Leslie's feelings about feeding her baby reflect her feelings about herself as a mother. One of the many great things about becoming a mother is the curative effect a baby can have on you as you get another chance to confront some difficult personal issues. Leslie's openness to change is an inspiration.

FOUR

Changes in Your Marriage
The Duet Becomes a Trio

"I feel more in love with my husband than ever. At times I am overwhelmed with passion for him. It is a wonderful time for us."

"I'm furious at my husband for not caring more, not participating more, not helping more. Sometimes the most insignificant things make all my anger well up inside of me and I just hate him."

These statements were both made by Nan about her husband, Rick, during the third and fourth months of new motherhood. Husbands and wives are often surprised at the intensity and range of feelings they have for one another during the first year of parenthood. Your feelings, too, may seem exaggerated and contradictory at times. Thoughts and behaviors that seem impossible to coexist do.

The transition to parenthood happens in fits and starts, with ups and downs and continual adjustments in your marriage along the way. It can be a time of deepening love and renewed commitment. It can be a time of extreme marital stress and even of crisis. It may well be the biggest challenge you face as a couple. Even the steadiest of husband-wife relationships will feel turbulence. Your successful navigation through this period does not necessarily depend on how long you have been married, whether or not your baby was planned, how you fared during pregnancy and childbirth, or on your financial situation. Instead, much depends on mutual respect, flexibility, and communication. Ultimately, a lot comes down to hard work, shared vision, and blind faith.

Many couples become especially close during the last months before their baby is due. Both man and woman project and dream about their baby-to-be and what parenthood will hold for them. If they attend childbirth classes, the man may develop a heightened appreciation for his wife. He may also feel grateful to have, at last, a role to play in the upcoming delivery. As she gets bigger and bigger, the woman may become increasingly dependent on her partner. The progression of the pregnancy, her growing belly and nervous excitement, the teamwork between husband and wife during childbirth, all climax with the arrival of the new baby.

You will probably find, as most couples do, that parenthood is a surprise package. It's not exactly what you expected, read, or talked about, or even what you hoped or feared it might be. Not only is a new little person developing before your eyes, you are being transformed as well. As small and helpless as your new baby is, he has the ability to cast powerful spells on your marital relationship as he brings out new facets in your personalities.

By the time we reach our discussion on marriage the group has been together for over a month. The women talk easily and openly and have come to depend on the group.

"Today we are going to talk about how parenthood has affected your marriages," we begin.

"I have to go now," Elizabeth says, and laughter fills the room.

It is not unusual to want to run and hide from the confusing changes that are taking place in your marriage. New feelings about your spouse are hard to confront. Strong negative ones are painful to accept. Change of any sort can be worrisome or frightening. A lot of women keep quiet, thinking they alone are guilty of murderous thoughts about their husbands. But as soon as one cat is out of the bag, many more follow. And as the women see themselves in the others' stories, their own feelings become less threatening, less overwhelming.

"My husband says we're not working as a team anymore. And he's right," Jessica comments.

"I thought my husband was more sensitive," says Leslie. But he's not acting like the man I married. He comes home late. I'm a wreck. And he actually sits down in front of the television as if nothing is wrong. He would never have done that before the baby. It makes me so sad."

"Our love life was good before the baby," says Elizabeth. "Even through most of the pregnancy. But now, if he tells me one more time that he's 'patiently waiting for some good loving,' I'll scream."

Maggie sums it up succinctly, saying, "This baby has totally transformed our lives!"

As parents, you will have to adjust to new levels of stress and fatigue, a new kind of social life and even a new sex life. Your focus, your needs and ability to give to one another will change. Your interests, concerns, and conversations will change. Feelings about time and money will change. The division of labor in your house, as well as the balance of power between you and your partner, will change. Given the all-encompassing nature of this life transition, it makes sense that couples will struggle as they adjust to parenthood.

"At times it is intensely competitive between us. It's as if we are both keeping silent scores," says Nan.

The early weeks and months of new parenthood can seem like a blur, a wild run of emotions. Life is in upheaval, your marriage is stressed, but often little is said or done about it. Consumed with the care and growing love for their babies, new mothers often feel sequestered from the rest of the world, lonely and overwhelmed by all the changes in their lives. Often new fathers say they don't know how to act at home anymore. At day's end, both husband and wife crash with exhaustion, knowing something feels wrong but too tired or confused to talk about it. When asked to describe their marriages in these initial months of new parenthood, comments from the mothers in our groups range from "We're sailing" to "We're drowning." Most agree that the waters are choppy.

Perhaps the greatest pressure on new parents is trying to live up to the romantic image of happiness and harmony that a new baby is supposed to bring. It is a myth that, as parents, you and your husband will automatically feel more in love, more deeply bonded to one another, fulfilled and happy. Because everyone around you seems to expect you to be basking in new love, it becomes especially difficult to handle the bad feelings you may be having.

"We are both stretched to our limits," says Nan. "We are both working long, hard days. He rarely gets to see the baby. It's not his fault, I know, but it makes me angry."

"There's lots more tension between us. I snap like that," says Maggie, clicking her fingers.

A baby *can* bring a husband and wife together, swelling their love with new pride and affirming their bond. But a lot of these good feelings can be dampened by anger and resentment as the stresses of new parenthood play themselves out. More commonly, you may alternate between one day feeling alienated from your spouse, another day, newly and deeply close. Jealousy, competition, tension and judgmental feelings are all common, but they can feel especially threatening to new parents who expected a more rosy time of family life. It can be liberating to let go of the myth of the new, happy family, to work toward realistic expectations for each other and to begin again to be in love.

"There is a definite *Before* and *After* feel to my relationship with my husband," says Jessica. "Most of the time I wish we had the *Before* back."

Though you may ache for the simplicity of it, you cannot realistically strive to go back to anything resembling the *Before*. You have to make something new—a family.

"I am forced to be the practical person, to be totally in

charge of Nell, thinking ahead, taking care of details, making sure we have what we need. Greg has much more freedom, so of course he can be more relaxed," says Jessica about her husband, who is a university professor. "So he's the starved romantic and I've become the drone and the nag."

While there is a certain amount of humor in Jessica's description of herself, it is clear that she is not happy with her own behavior and that she resents her husband for not assuming more responsibility for Nell.

"My biggest worry right now is that I feel like I have nothing interesting to talk about with David," says Ronnie about her husband, who is a lawyer with a small firm. "Dinner has always been our time for each other. Now there's a painful lack of conversation. My day revolves around diapers and feedings and, it's strange, but I don't know what else to talk about. I think David resents all the baby talk so I try not to talk about Elyse, and then we are left feeling this distance between us."

"You know, I think Ethan and I had less connection before the baby," says Jane. "We used to be on such separate tracks. But now we have a common interest—Justin. He has done more good for our marriage than anything else."

"Jonathan and I have been talking a lot about him taking care of Lucy either full-time or part-time after she is one year old," says Elizabeth. "Just that awareness seems to make a difference between us. Like we're in it together."

Some couples do bond together in a new way, as Jane and Ethan did, merging with a common focus. As often, however, the paths and roles of husband and wife as father and mother begin to diverge. The arrival of a new baby demands a major reshuffling and reorganization of responsibilities and roles for a couple. This, in itself, necessitates some adjustment. But beneath the logistical, domestic changes is the shifting of attentions and affections going on within the new family. New love alliances are forming and these alter the emotional balance of your marriage.

✑ THE TRIANGLE

How would you feel if your husband fell in love with another person? How would you feel if you fell in love with someone new? The tricky part about having a baby is that both husband and wife *are* falling in love with a new person—their baby. Their once exclusive, eyes-for-you-only relationship has become a triangle.

"Saturday morning I got up early with Justin and brought him into bed with us," Jane tells the group. "Ethan was still asleep on his stomach with a pillow over his head. I was cooing and cuddling with Justin. I whispered to him, 'Who's my best boy?' and Ethan's hand shot up. It kind of broke my heart."

This image brings forth a mixture of sympathetic sighs and laughter from the other mothers. Elizabeth adds her version of the same story. "When Jonathan was on his way out the door to go to work yesterday morning, I was still in my nightgown, nursing Lucy on the couch. He had said good-bye to us and then from the doorway, he turned around and said in a sweet, little voice, 'I'm jealous.'"

"I empathize with Jonathan," Nan says. "Emma is the new love of Rick's life. When Rick comes home from work he always kisses Emma first. I know this sounds silly, but it makes me feel forgotten."

"That who-gets-the-first-kiss debate has come up for me and my husband, too," says Alicia. "I'm guilty I know, but by the time I get home from work I'm physically aching to see my baby. It's not about loving one more than the other, but I guess it feels that way to Alan."

The new love alliances created by your baby are bound to create jealousies, hurt feelings, and misunderstandings between you and your husband. These responses are hard to own up to and sometimes communication will shut down as a result. The balances you had created in your marriage before the baby, the compromises, understandings, forgivenesses, autonomies, and dependencies, no longer seem to apply.

"Often Vince doesn't get home from work until 7:00 P.M.," says Leslie. "By that time Eric's in his worst state of the day, and when Vince holds him he cries more. I know Vince is taking it personally. He passes Eric back to me with a look of defeat. I feel bad for him, but I have to admit that part of me feels glad that the baby is choosing me."

"I'm amazed at how quickly my allegiances have shifted," says Nan. "Rick is home with the flu right now. Before the baby when he would get sick I used to dote on him. I'd get him orange juice and sit with him and, well—baby him. Now it's 'Here's the Sudafed.' "

"I feel totally caught up with Sarah," says Marta. "It's hard for me to even conceive of the demands of a husband as well. I would have a hard time splitting myself like that. But I worry sometimes that I'll never be able to make room for another relationship."

"To be perfectly honest, I *am* more interested in my baby than in my husband these days," Elizabeth admits.

Some new mothers describe the powerfully consuming connection to their babies as bordering on the obsessional. This absorption with the baby is a natural and important phenomenon in the development of the mother-baby relationship, especially in the first year. But this bond can feel exclusive, especially if the father is not made a part of the triangle in an intimate way. A father's ability to understand and accept this intense mother-child connection is important to the adjustment of becoming a family. But as important is the couple's ability to stay connected in a loving way as husband and wife.

⟳ BUTTING OUT

"I know why my husband backs off from helping me with Jack," says Maggie. "I can't help it but I find myself correcting him all the time. 'You put the outfit on backward. The diaper is on too tight. Hold him more securely in the bathtub. More gently when he is taking a bottle.' I'd back off if he talked to me like that."

Most mothers describe themselves as desperate for a more equal sharing of the work of parenthood with their spouse. Yet these same women explain that they often are unable to let go of the controls. Fathers confirm that the more they are watched and negatively judged, the less adequate they feel, the less well they perform, and the less inclined they feel to jump in and do the job. It can be hard to watch your husband fumbling with the baby's diaper or to see him respond in a less than perfectly attuned way. But it is important for women to realize that it's alright for their husbands to do things differently. So, bite your tongue, tie your hands, keep your eyeballs from rolling, or simply leave the house so that your husband has the chance to make his own mistakes. It is critical for new fathers to build their own expertise in their baby's care and their confidence in this new relationship. Some husbands need to be actively encouraged to take their rightful place as parent. But once they are more involved with their baby's care they become both more adept and more attuned with their child. And with you. The flip side of this coin is when a father assumes the role of primary caretaker and the mother returns to the work world. These women may cringe with envy at the easy, everyday relationship between father and child.

Many marital problems arise not for lack of love, but over the daily chores. Often housework becomes the focus of arguments between a husband and wife after a baby is born. When asked how the division of labor at home had changed since the baby's arrival, Leslie responded, "I am the Division of Labor."

Jessica adds, "I thought Greg said he would take on fifty percent of the housework. But now I'm thinking maybe he said fifteen percent. When I ask him to help me around the house now he says, 'I work all day.'"

Many men go into a "Great Provider" mode during the early months of their baby's life. They become more driven, feel more responsible, and often more anxious. They work longer hours and become more preoccupied with their jobs. Many new fathers talk about the heightened sense of needing to succeed, of no longer having time to experiment with their careers, of needing to establish and meet goals more quickly. It may seem like these men are shying away from the intimacy of home life or shirking their share of duties in the house and with baby care. But when questioned, these men speak more about their overwhelming feelings of responsibility toward their new families and their worries about money. The pressures of the traditional role of father-as-breadwinner surface in the most modern of families.

"In my marriage the roles have become so set and so separate," says Leslie. "Vince gets up early to leave for the office, works really hard, and comes home late. I take care of Eric and everything else at home. But Vince says to me at the end of the day, 'Every time I come home the baby is crying and the house is a mess and you are in a terrible mood.' And he's right. It all causes such scowling and bitching between us. I don't even know what I want from Vince. I guess a break now and then or more respect for what I am doing."

"Get Vince to take care of Eric all day one Saturday," Jessica suggests to Leslie. "It worked for me. Last weekend I went out for almost four hours and Greg took care of Nell. When I came home Greg was exhausted and said, 'I can't believe you do this all day every day!' That felt good."

Jane says, "I have to defend men here a little bit. Ethan's not like some men I know, who want to stay home with the baby, but he has been pulling his weight. On top of his work, he's been doing all of the shopping and cooking since Justin was born."

Stepping away from the primary role with your baby and allowing your husband to fill that spot on a regular basis will strengthen your marital relationship and help to balance the division of labor in your home. It will give your husband newfound respect for the work you do and

it offers him the chance to connect with his baby in a
more intimate way.

∾ SEX AND ROMANCE

Nervous laughter is the response when we first question
the women in our group about their sex lives. It doesn't
take long, however, for them to get right to the heart of
the matter.

"My husband is grumpy and horny. I'm bitchy and
overtired. It's all very romantic," says Leslie.

"I'm so aware of Lucy in her nursery," says Elizabeth,
"that I cannot relax enough to begin to make love."

Nan says, "At the end of every single fight we have—
whether it's about the baby, the housework, money, his
work schedule, or my exhaustion, when we finally get to
the real issue, it almost always revolves around sex. He
wants it, and I don't have the desire. Mentally or physically. Then I feel like we've hit a brick wall."

As a couple's love song turns from a duet to a trio,
many complain that the passion and the romance, the ten-
derness and compassion have seeped out of their relationship. What happens to desire between husband and wife
after their first baby is born? For some, it goes under-
ground like a submerged river, cutting a new bed in
which to flow for a while. For some, it can dry up altogether. For others, desire will remain or even increase,
flooding over and bathing everyday relations with new
vitality.

"I feel more attracted to my husband," says Ronnie.
"We make love more than we used to. Being parents

makes our relationship so solid and so free at the same time. I guess that makes me feel sexy."

"I'm definitely more in love with my husband," says Jane. "And our sex life is great. When we get to it."

"Greg and I used to have a hot sex life," says Jessica. "He was the professor of a course I was taking and by the time I had finished the final exam, there was electricity between us. It was a very passionate relationship. We met in the afternoon to make love. Now it's like I'm a different person. I feel self-conscious. I can't relax."

The transition to parenthood can be even more difficult if a relationship had originally been highly charged sexually and romantically. The loss may seem more profound, the changes more obvious, the sacrifice more difficult.

"We couldn't have sex during the last trimester of my pregnancy. And then we waited six weeks after Emma was born," says Nan. "That's close to five months! I don't think I remember how."

While some women report increased sexual desire and satisfaction during pregnancy, typically sexual relations will diminish during these months. Following the birth of a baby the sex life of new parents is temporarily on hold. The mother has undergone a major physical feat; roughly fifteen percent of mothers have had major surgery.

Depending on the type of delivery, vaginal or C-section, the amount of tearing or the need for an episiotomy, recovery time can last anywhere from six weeks to six months. Additionally, postpartum hormonal changes affect the mother both physically and emotionally. Up to ten percent of new mothers experience postpartum depression. The return to sexual relations presents challenges for most couples.

Maggie is twisting Jack's blanket in her hands as she

asks, "Is anyone else having trouble with intercourse? It's been a little painful for me. It never was before."

Maggie's question elicits a chorus of groans from the group. Elizabeth adds, "Painful? I wouldn't know. I tell him to keep that thing away from me."

Unfortunately, many women are not forewarned by their obstetricians or by the literature that sex is usually uncomfortable and sometimes painful even after the typical six-week postpartum waiting period. Hormonal changes make the vaginal opening and walls tighter and drier. Mothers who breast-feed report decreased vaginal lubrication for as long as up to six months. Some women tear internally during childbirth and the resulting scar tissue can affect their enjoyment of sex. If an episiotomy was required, the perineum may still be sore even after the incision has healed.

It may take several attempts over several weeks of trying before you are able to fully engage in intercourse. You and your partner should know that it may take time to achieve full penetration comfortably. K-Y jelly or some other water-based lubricant can help. After a vaginal delivery, the size and position of a woman's uterus has changed. You may notice a change in what feels good for you, and trying different positions may help this.

The hiatus in sexual relations, for whatever reasons, can turn into interpersonal tension if left undiscussed. Often couples find themselves in adversarial positions, one wanting, the other denying. Patience and care during sex and talking openly with your partner will help. Intercourse will gradually start to feel good again as you engage in it more regularly. It is important to go at your own pace and to be gentle with one another. As you are working toward comfortable lovemaking, remember that sexual and sensual pleasure can be achieved in many ways.

Jessica looks agitated. "It's been three months since I gave birth and I'm still not comfortable having sex. I asked my midwife about it and she said, 'Take your time.' Then I asked a friend who is a gynecologist and she said not to worry, that it would improve. Everyone else seems so calm about it. But I'm really worried."

Typically, the waiting period for postpartum intercourse is six weeks after delivery. But everyone is different and personal timetables vary. We've known women who were able to have intercourse comfortably six weeks after delivery and others who were not able to fully enjoy sex until six months after the birth of their babies. For some women the emotional aftereffects of giving birth can be as real as the physical pain, and this, too, will impact on the ease and enjoyment of sex. For many the pain of intercourse is reminiscent of labor and may be upsetting. So if you, like Jessica, are worried about your lack of comfort with sex since having your baby, remember, it can take some women months to accept the extraordinary drama of childbirth.

"When I get home I play with Keith, make dinner, and then Alan gets home and we get a chance to visit," says Alicia. "We try to catch up on each other's days, but Keith tends to take over. Then by the time I put the baby to bed, Alan and I are both ready for bed too. Sometimes we look longingly into each other's eyes and then we both fall asleep."

Most parents, and especially mothers, experience the effects of sleep deprivation in the first few months of new parenthood. Exhaustion decreases libido or sexual drive. Continually disrupted sleep may leave you slowed down, confused, out of sorts, depressed. But as time goes by, your baby's sleeping patterns will become more regular, and as you get more sleep and your fatigue lessens, sexual drive should increase.

"I can't even blame tiredness," says Nan. "I feel loving and close with Rick but I don't want to make love with him the way I used to. What's even weirder is that I don't really miss it. Emma gets more of me these days than Rick does."

Nan's experience is not as unusual as she thinks. Many new mothers report a decrease in sexual desire for their partners, which seems, in part, to be linked to the physical nature of caring for a baby. The mother-child relationship can fulfill many physical and emotional needs for a woman. Feeding, kissing, holding, touching, and all the skin-to-skin contact that is natural in the daily care of a baby can be very sensual. After a full day of being with a baby, sexual gratification may seem unnecessary.

"I love to lie in the grass with him or take a bath together. When we put our faces together he sucks my chin. I kiss his stomach and he laughs. I've never been so happy," says Jane.

Jane is not describing her marital love life but her maternal one. She is in the process of falling in love with her baby and there is a romance about it which is very intense. Some husbands share in the romance and love of their new baby. Others derive pleasure watching their wives as mothers. But other men find this love relationship threatening. Though provocative, the "romance" between a mother and baby is not only normal, it is a critically important element of a child's early development.

"There have been times since I split up with my husband when I've yearned to be close with a man," says Marta. "But since Sarah came into my life I don't feel that as much anymore. She's such good company. And it's nice because I can love her as much as I want to. Sometimes that's a little scary actually."

Many single mothers fear they may become overly dependent on their children for a sense of intimacy and closeness. This can be especially confusing in the early months, when the mother-child relationship tends to be all-consuming. Marta is aware that she doesn't want her baby to be a stand-in for a mature love relationship and we encourage her to enjoy the positive and healthy feelings of love she has for Sarah. What Marta's fears point out for everyone is that the marital relationship can provide an important balance and sense of stability to a mother while she falls in love with her baby.

One of the most common outcries of new parents is that the spontaneity has gone from their marriage. They can no longer decide at the last minute to go out to a movie for coffee or an afternoon stroll. Time doesn't unfold magically for them anymore and it is easy to get into a rut of staying home, taking care of the baby, and making sleep a priority.

It is extremely important to set aside time to be alone with your husband. A regular night out together once a week or once every two weeks can become a treasured routine. Only regular time together for fun and relaxation will revive the feelings of intimacy and romance so many couples say they lack.

Elizabeth says, "I got a baby-sitter for the first time when Lucy was two months old so Jonathan and I could go out on a date. Being alone together reminded me of how close our relationship really is."

"My husband wants to go out on a date. But I don't want to leave the baby. I just don't feel ready," says Jessica.

Sometimes a woman will admit that she is actually avoiding that first date, afraid to confront the built-up tensions and disappointments that have grown between her and her partner. But a date can be exactly what is needed to break a bad cycle. If you are finding a dozen reasons why you don't have time to be alone with your husband, it's time to evaluate why.

"It must be particularly difficult because Nell cries so much to feel alright about leaving her," says Alicia to Jessica. "But I think the hard part is making that first break. I get so little time with Keith that I really dragged my feet about that. But when Alan and I went out on our first date it was wonderful. We didn't stay out long but it made us realize we wanted and needed to do it more often."

"My first date was a fiasco," says Nan. "Rick and I went out to the movies and an hour into it my milk came in. I suddenly became desperate to go home. I started looking at my watch every five minutes. Rick tried to calm me down, and I burst into tears. I ran to the telephone and called to check on Emma. My father-in-law told me she was fine, not to worry, to have a good time. I forced myself to sit through the rest of the movie, but it was torture. Before we were even out of the theater Rick and I were fighting.

"I know I ruined that first date and that Rick was disappointed. It's just that I've been so connected to the baby for so long that it feels terrible to be disconnected. It's not just the two months she's been with us. It's the whole pregnancy, too."

It can be hard to engage with your spouse when much of you remains with your baby. Sometimes it is best to plan a short outing for a first date so the pressure is not on full steam. Each time, leaving your baby will get a little easier. And when your baby starts to sleep longer at night it will be easier to spend personal time *awake* with your husband on a regular basis. In fact, from all accounts, it is immeasurably helpful and strengthening to the marital relationship.

One of the most important tasks of early parenthood is to balance your attachment to your baby with the bonds of your marriage. Your marital relationship is vitally important to all three of you. If you and your husband make your marriage a priority, the whole family will benefit.

∾ LOVER AND MOTHER

"It's been a very sensual time for me," says Ronnie. "I go from breast feeding the baby in her room back into a warm bed to make love with my husband. It all feels delicious."

Now that you have a baby your self-image begins to broaden, incorporating the idea of Mother with Wife and Lover. Some women find this process a natural, enjoyable one. But many find the pulls of motherhood challenging to the marital relationship, especially in the beginning. The roles of mother and lover seem to be at odds with one another; the changed orientation from sexual woman to nurturing mother a one-way street. For example, if your breasts were an important erogenous zone in sexual play with your husband before the baby, it can be confusing if you are breast-feeding. A nursing mother may feel inhibited if milk leaks from her breasts during foreplay. She may feel jolted out of her sexual frame of mind. Her husband may feel, "Are these breasts mine or the baby's?"

"My husband brought me a present the other night," says Jessica. "I melted. Then when I opened it, my heart fell. He'd gone out and bought a lacy, sexy thing. It was the last thing on earth I felt like getting. I was embarrassed to even think about putting it on this body. I didn't know how to react. So I made light of it. I couldn't let him know how I was really feeling."

One woman might enjoy a gift which affirms she is still sexy and attractive to her partner. But for another, putting on something silky or slinky can feel ludicrous, especially if she is still overweight, engorged, and used to wearing a nursing bra to bed at night. A sexy nightgown may not have been the gift that Jessica hoped for, but for Greg it was his way of telling Jessica that she is as desirable and sexually attractive to him as ever. We understand Jessica's reticence to confront her husband with her true reaction to the nightgown. Honest communication about sexuality is difficult for most couples. But staying silent will only widen the gap between them. If Jessica and Greg can discuss the changes in their sexual feelings it can be an opportunity for renewed closeness.

∾ HOW TO TACKLE CHANGE

The marital relationship is the foundation on which a baby grows. New parents, however, naturally focus their attention and energies on their infant, and sometimes to the neglect of one another. The romantic feelings and sexual passion that created this very baby may retreat in the face of so much change. One tiny baby can create one big power struggle between a husband and wife.

Marriage requires upkeep, patience, and honest communication. There are many ways to put energy into your marriage, to foster romance, reignite passion, restore the balance and fun in your relationship with your spouse. The women with whom we have worked over the last eight years have each come face-to-face with the challenge of keeping their marriages strong and romantic in the company of a new baby. They have talked openly with us and each other about what has worked for them. Here are some of their experiences and ideas:

- "Spend time *alone* with your husband. Go out for coffee, dinner, or for a long walk together. You might want to bring the baby along, and that's nice sometimes, but it's a very different thing to be out alone with your husband."

- "Every couple with children we know had told us to set a regular weekly date. So we did. But it felt like a luxury. We had never gone out once a week *before* the baby. So we put it off and then suddenly we realized a whole month had gone by. So we tried again with once a week. It still feels like a luxury. But a really important one."

- "Find a good baby-sitter! It's worth every penny."

- "Don't expect your husband to read your mind. *Tell* him what you are thinking and how you are feeling."

- "I get so caught up with everything I have to do that I'm running all the time. I don't know how to stop. So my advice to myself is—Stop for a minute every day and look into my husband's eyes."

- "Almost my favorite thing to do with my husband is to read out loud together. We've always done that. We were going through a rough stretch and I was reading a book on marriage. I suggested we read it out loud together and his response was 'Don't enlist the experts against me!' I kept bugging him about it until he gave in. And he admitted later that it was useful. It is a good way to start talking."

- "I'm a bit of a sentimental sap, but every so often I get out our honeymoon album and sit on the couch with my husband and we look at it together. It reminds us of all the reasons we fell in love, the reasons we chose each other. It puts us in that courting mood again."

- "Things had to get pretty bad before my husband and I agreed to go, but marriage counseling helped us. We learned more about each other in six months than in the four years we had been together. The hardest thing the therapist tried to get us to do was to listen to each other without getting defensive. That seems simple, but it's not. It's almost impossible for me. Especially when my husband is being critical. I want to fight back. But I do this trick with myself. I tell myself, 'Just listen to what he wants to say.' There's almost always a kernel of truth in it. And it's liberating for me to be able to tell him when something is bothering me without getting into a fight."

- "One night after the baby was asleep my husband was taking a shower. I got in with him and it was so nice. Like old times. I highly recommend it."

- "The best thing we did for ourselves was to go on an overnight trip. I have it easy because my parents live nearby and they are great with the baby. My husband and I went to a funny little bed-and-breakfast on Long Island. The next morning it was like waking up on our honeymoon."

- "By the time the baby is asleep at night the ONLY thing I want to do is to go to sleep. I have no energy or desire to make love at night. The first time we made love in the afternoon during the baby's nap was like a new experience. I was actually awake for it."

- "Do something physical and fun, like tennis or bowling or dancing."

- "We got into a routine of always taking turns taking care of the baby. But we never saw each other. So now every other Sunday we all go to the zoo or the park. It feels very old-fashioned and wonderful. It's like we are creating ourselves as a family."

- "Take time for yourself and get your husband to take time for himself, too. Go to the gym, get a haircut, go to a movie, visit a friend. You deserve it."

- "My mother's advice to me about marriage has always been 'Take your time. Don't expect things to happen overnight.' That's probably because whenever things get strained between me and my husband I want to fix it fast. When I accept the idea that relationships change slowly, I feel much calmer and more confident about my marriage."

These pieces of advice speak to the typical stresses experienced by most couples after the birth of their first child. There are marriages, however, that become more seriously distressed, particularly those that were shaky before parenthood. When the gulf in communication or the level of fighting between you and your spouse feels as if it is jeopardizing the viability of the marriage, do not assume that things will get better on their own. Even though it may feel like a frightening step to take, the time is right to seek the help of a professional. A marriage counselor can assess the degree of seriousness in your marital discord and guide you through this time. Marriage therapy can help you to untangle confusing emotions and learn skills for more productive and loving communication.

One Man's Story

To help you to better understand your husband, to add the male point of view to the mother's circle for a moment, we interviewed many of the husbands of our group members. Of course, everyone is unique in his perspective and circumstances, but we think Rick speaks for a great many men. We hope his story may inspire you and your husband to have the important conversations that may be needed in your relationship.

"I used to feel so in tune with Nan," Rick begins. "Now I don't know what she is thinking about or even why she is so upset all the time. Every night before I walk through the door I say a small prayer to myself. 'Please, make her normal again.'

"Nan says I do things wrong with the baby all the time. Even when it's something as simple as putting on Emma's pajamas. If the baby lets out the slightest cry, Nan will storm in and take over. I'm left with my tail between my legs.

"I'm trying to be a good father and a good husband, but according to Nan, I'm always thinking of myself instead of the baby. When she says, 'You don't care enough' or 'You don't have enough patience' these are code things which mean 'Back off. I'm in charge.' It makes it hard to even discuss. It's tough for me. Very tough.

"The pressure is really on now. The money is there but with little to spare. I don't think Nan respects what it means for me to be the one breadwinner of the family.

"Family life intrudes into my work life in a way I never anticipated. Throughout my workday I have many more telephone conversations with Nan than I ever used to. She must think I'm not really working that hard, that I'm having a social time with my coworkers and that there are no stresses. She wants me home by five-thirty. No discussion. But that's almost impossible for me. If anything, I have to work harder than ever now that we have a baby.

"Now that we have a baby it seems like we're running, running, running from morning to night," Rick continues. "Life has changed in so many ways. There is less time for work, play, pleasure, relaxation.

"When I come home from work, Nan greets me with a list of demands. It might have been a brutal day but that doesn't seem to matter. It's my turn to take the baby, get the toilet paper, make dinner, change the diaper.

"According to Nan, my free time is my time at work.

In her mind, when I'm home I'm hers. I'd like to see some of my friends occasionally. I'd like her to see her friends for that matter. But I know I'd have to really fight for it. If I had two hours in the evening once a week to myself, that would go a long way. And I know she needs that as well. She never takes time for herself. She should take more care of herself instead of taking her frustrations out on me.

"I know we need time alone together but she says she doesn't trust anyone to baby-sit right now. Granted there are certain things she can do better than anyone. Like calm down the baby when she's crying. But Emma is almost three months old. When I push Nan on this one, she gets very upset. So what do we do—never go out again?

"To me Nan is as desirable as ever. I'm very attracted to her. And I tell her that. But she's self-conscious about her body now. There was a time when she'd walk across our bedroom naked. But that's a thing of the past, and I miss it.

"Our sex life has changed dramatically. That's been very tough. We've had less and less sex. I want it more than she does. But I don't want to have to ask for it all the time. And I can't bear it when I get the sense that she is only making love because she feels bad for me. I understand that she still feels a little sore, that she's having hormonal and emotional changes, but I don't accept the lack of understanding of my desires. I wish she would give me a chance to feel closer. Even the basic pampering is gone. She is less responsive, less affectionate. An occasional 'I love you' would be nice. In some ways I resent the baby for taking her away from me.

"I don't really have anyone else to talk to about all this stuff. I have a few friends who are fathers and we joke about the afternoon phone calls to the office that start, 'When are you coming home tonight?' And we joke about the lack of sex. But we don't talk about what is really going on.

"I can't even talk to Nan about my feelings about sex without her becoming defensive. I have desires that need to be met and they are simply not addressed. I'm in this marriage for the long term and, despite the changes, I still love Nan, so I'm not overly worried. But if things were to continue like this for a long time, I wouldn't be so sure. Things will have to change.

"We planned an overnight getaway. Or rather, I planned it. She resisted every step of the way. When her sister said she'd take care of the baby Nan finally agreed. But I knew she was only trying to please me. The trip turned into a nightmare. All she wanted to do was go home. So we cut it short.

"On the drive home we sat in stony silence. When we got home Nan had her tearful reunion with Emma and realized the baby was fine. When Emma was napping later we finally had our first serious talk about what was really going on between us. It was a long emotional talk. We both cried. I told her I didn't want to take the trip just for me. I wanted to take it for us. I wanted to have fun together again. And I was able to tell her how frustrated I feel about never having sex anymore. It was the first time she listened without responding negatively. And she told me some things I hadn't realized. She said that a lot of her worries about leaving the baby have to do with her mother's death. Even though it has been four years, she has been very sad and confused about that. Being away actually made that very clear to her and she felt she could work on that. I hope our talk was a turning point for us. In any case it helped just to understand each other better."

For Nan and Rick there was a long period of poor communication and brewing resentment before an honest exchange was possible. It is common for new parents to be so stunned by the arrival of their child, so hurt or surprised by each other's reactions, and so unsure of what to expect or about how to proceed that much is left unsaid. Enormous stresses can build and for some, only big, emotionally loaded fights can let out these pent-up feelings. Even arguments can be helpful if you and your husband are good at making up and untangling the real issues from the more obvious surface problems. More helpful than the occasional dam-bursting fight, however, are the small discussions, the little concessions, the minor adjustments and tinkerings that you can accomplish on a daily basis.

Becoming a parent is a landmark event in life. It opens a whole new chapter of adulthood and new dimensions in your relationship with your husband. The joys and the responsibilities of raising children together will carve your personalities and reshape your marriage forever.

At its best, marriage can provide deep intimacy, mutual support and appreciation, and a cherished soul mate. Keeping this kind of closeness alive once you have a child requires attention and care. If you begin with the idea that turmoil is common and that most new parents are doing marital battle in one form or another during the first year of parenthood, you might feel less overwhelmed or defeated and can help yourself and each other. It is important to understand the complexities of the changes in your marriage and not to underestimate the profound personal changes that by necessity take place as you turn from a couple into a family.

By the time your baby first stands up on his own, you and your husband should be feeling more surefooted yourselves. It can, and often does, take upwards of twelve months to assume your new roles, to settle into family life, and finally to have the energy, perspective, and enthusiasm to return to each other. From there, maintaining a happy and loving relationship with your husband as parents and partners is a lifelong process.

FIVE

Changes
in Your Body
The Journey
to Motherhood

"Being fat and pregnant is okay," says Jessica. "But just being fat isn't."

Most of the women nod in agreement as they cautiously eye one another.

"I love being a mother but I never wanted to look like one," says Elizabeth, adding, "I want my old body back."

"My husband says I look good. But the truth is, I hate the way my body looks right now," says Nan.

Women have a distinctly subjective relationship with their bodies. No matter what their weight, they *feel* fat or they *feel* thin. No matter what their look, they *feel* pretty or plain, graceful or awkward, sexy or not. To a great extent, a woman's self-image mirrors her body image.

Having given birth, the new mother does get her body back. But it has changed. She may stare in disbelief at her hips, stomach, or breasts, having thought they would have returned to their original, prepregnancy proportions.

She may feel uncomfortably big and describe herself as "fat." Her reactions are based in part on what she sees in the mirror, but they also reflect vestigial feelings about her body which date back to childhood, adolescence, and young adulthood.

Most young women do not feel satisfied with their looks and their figures. This is understandable given the enormous pressure American society puts on females to be thin and attractive, be it from the toy industry, the media, or the fashion world. Few women feel truly proud and at home in their own bodies. Few are free from self-criticism: breasts are too small or too large, legs are too short or too skinny, skin is too freckled, hair is too curly, thighs are too big, feet are ugly. From head to toe, the checklist continues, a personal evaluation based on story-book standards.

By their twenties and thirties men are generally more accepting of their bodies. But many women of this age live with an ongoing sense of falling short, and with some degree of secret shame and inadequacy based on their perception of their physical traits. So it is with an ear for this secret shame that we begin our discussion of the profound physical changes the new mothers have been through and how their bodies worked along the way. The journey includes attempts at conception, the nine growing months of pregnancy, the high drama of labor and child-birth, the tender, healing postpartum weeks, and the on-going changes in a woman's body during the first year of new motherhood.

Conceiving a baby is a leap of faith under any circum-stances. When a baby is not planned, lovemaking can ride a wave of passion and conception arrives on the shore out of breath, a surprise. When conception is a desired goal, intercourse becomes an act with a purpose. All of a sudden a woman's relationship with her body changes. She questions her body, does not know what to expect or when. Lovemaking becomes baby-making, mysterious and sober, full of anticipation and hope. It can sometimes be more stressful, sometimes more comical. A woman may monitor her temperature to gauge the fertile moment. She may meet her partner at odd hours of the day to try their luck. Some women speak of lying very still after intercourse to allow the sperm to swim freely. Others hold their feet up in the air, hoping gravity will help. Always there is the question: Will my body work?

"I'm thirty-five years old," Leslie begins. "I didn't have much time to fool around. My doctor said it could take up to a year to conceive. But I got pregnant right away. I was pleased and relieved and kind of proud. Vince felt so manly. I felt connected with my body in a way I never had before."

With age, health, fertility, and luck on your side, it can take anywhere from one to twelve months to conceive a first baby and sometimes longer. The chances of becoming pregnant lessen with age. And, once pregnant, the likelihood of miscarriage is between seventeen and twenty-five percent, again depending on age, something few people know or talk about. No matter what a woman's personal variables, trying to conceive a baby and carry it to term can have an unexpectedly strong, positive *or* negative impact on her self-image and self-esteem.

"I was so sure of myself," says Jessica, who at twenty-five is the youngest member of the group. "Greg and I decided we'd start trying ten months before our summer vacation so that the baby would come when we had time off. What a joke. We tried for almost a year. It became so stressful. We both felt guilty and angry. I felt like I was the failure but secretly hoped it was Greg. Neither one of us wanted to tell anyone.

"When we finally went to a specialist, it turned out it was me. I went on a fertility drug and three months later I got pregnant. By that time, though, I was so unsure of my body I was afraid something else would go wrong."

Marta, whose marriage ended largely because of the enormous stresses of infertility, sympathizes with Jessica.

"My husband and I started trying to get pregnant when I was thirty-two. We tried for almost three years. I would not believe that I couldn't get pregnant. Then, once I accepted the fact that there were problems, I wanted to try anything and everything. I pretended to be optimistic but I felt so disappointed and angry at my body. I was on the verge of tears all the time. And in the end, not only did my body fail, but my marriage failed too.

"It has taken a long time to feel better about myself," Marta continues. "I mean, when you are young, no one says that there is a chance you might not be able to have babies when you grow up. I always assumed I would be a mother one day. But I never expected to be a single, adoptive mother. I'm still disappointed in my body, but now that I have Sarah it doesn't matter so much anymore."

✑ GIRLHOOD

Like Marta, most females assume that becoming a mother is their right. In fact, at some point all little girls playact or fantasize about having babies. Preschool-age children create and project their own future roles with an absolute and wondrous confidence. When they are as young as three years old, girls begin to think about and personalize pregnancy and motherhood.

"In my last month of pregnancy," Jessica tells us, "my four-year-old niece said to me, 'When *I* grow up to be a mommy my baby will be a girl baby. Then my baby and your baby can be friends.' She had it all worked out!"

A little girl with a pregnant mother, aunt, or family friend can show astounding powers of mimicry. She will stuff her shirt with a pillow, arch and support her aching back, rest her hands on top of her belly, and shuffle along through an imaginary grown-up world talking about how she can feel her baby kick. A little girl who has watched a woman nurse may gently hold a toy animal or doll to her own chest and explain that her baby is hungry.

This playacting exemplifies the early years, when a child usually feels tremendous confidence and exhuberance in her body and what it can do. She has infinite joy in the physicality of everyday life. A girl's vivid identification with her own mother naturally leads her to believe that she can and will one day be pregnant and have a baby too.

∽ ADOLESCENCE

With the onset of menstruation, a girl is made more aware of her body. Hormonal and physical changes during puberty and an emerging sense of sexuality can make her feel awkward, confused, and self-conscious. Even the most self-assured young girl will have ambivalent feelings about her body during adolescence. When asked about their teenage years, many women say they were consumed with dieting. Almost all remember being preoccupied with their figures, skin, and hair. Some say they were ashamed of their bodies' new curves, new cycles, and new smells.

How a teenage girl feels about her body is also influenced by the messages she receives from her family during this time of budding sexuality. If a girl's father or mother is uncomfortable with their daughter's new shape or if a sibling taunts and mocks her, she will probably think there is something bad about her body. If a girl's father, brother, or other male is inappropriately attentive she may feel at once flattered, confused, threatened, and humiliated. And if a girl is the victim of sexual abuse, it can take decades to regain any sense of pride about and acceptance of her own body.

Parents who respect their daughter's maturation help her both to accept the changes in her body and to be proud of herself. A parent who is sensitive to a young girl's feelings about getting her first menstrual period, for example, will help her to understand that she is going through important physical and emotional changes, that she is growing up. Recognition, even celebration, of this female rite of passage affirms its significance for a young girl.

"I vividly remember the day I first got my period," says Ronnie. "My parents congratulated me! I remember being a little embarrassed at all their attention, but it made me feel special too. I remember my parents whispering to one another and then telling me that I had become a young lady and they wanted to give me a special present. They handed me a long, thin box. It was a beautiful silver necklace. My father told me that it had been his mother's. It made me feel so grown up."

∽ PREGNANCY

During pregnancy some women feel more beautiful and womanly than ever. Some feel they are in an altered state. Not since puberty has your body undergone such dramatic change and growth. Not since adolescence have you had to redefine yourself specifically by the changes in your body.

"When I look back on this past year, I can't believe what my body has been through," says Jane.

Then Jane covers Justin's ears and, lowering her voice to a whisper, says, "It was like being inhabited by an alien. My body exploded. I gained sixty pounds. I was nauseated all the time. I felt totally out of control."

"My feet and ankles swelled so much that I couldn't fit into my shoes," says Elizabeth. "I was very uncomfortable. But even so, I miss being pregnant. It was amazing to have a life growing inside of me."

From the comical to the sublime, the pregnant state is both exaggerated and miraculous. Some women carry completely in their belly but for many, the whole landscape of the body changes as it swells and grows. In addition, pregnancy can cause nausea, indigestion, fatigue, the constant need to urinate, backaches, varicose veins, hemorrhoids, and stretch marks. A pregnant woman may experience shortness of breath as her diaphragm becomes crowded. She may feel strong contractions or kicks from her growing baby. Then, there are those women who experience very few of these physical effects and seem to sail through their pregnancies. They feel strong and energized. Or spiritual and womanly. They "glow" and have an overall sense of physical well-being.

The importance of eating well during pregnancy can offer a welcome break to women whose lives were dominated by dieting. For those with a history of weight problems or eating disorders, the need to eat more and more frequently can sometimes trigger anxiety. Some women won't allow themselves to eat the way they should or, alternatively, the prospect of unavoidable weight gain can result in binge behavior.

Leslie, who had spoken privately with us two weeks earlier about her eating disorder, now tells the group that she was anorexic as a teenager. "Body image and self-image are definitely all mixed up for me," Leslie says. "I've had to really struggle to feel good about my body. I was in therapy when I was younger and I overcame a lot of my eating problems. Getting pregnant was actually a great thing for me. And it happened so easily. I was very happy my body worked that way. I felt terrific during the first trimester. But when I started to really put on weight, I couldn't handle it. I got on the scale several times a day and I got so anxious I practically stopped eating. My OB sat me down and spoke very seriously with me at that point. She gave me a very specific diet to follow and told me that *she* would keep the record of my weight gain. I was not to look at the scale again for the rest of my pregnancy. I trusted her and her plan worked. I got back on track. But I still struggle with certain issues."

The other women listen with empathy and interest. Leslie seems relieved to tell her story. Marta comments that getting rid of the bathroom scale would probably be a positive move for most women. And Nan says that although she never had a full-blown eating disorder, she has struggled with her weight and bad feelings about herself. In almost every mothers' group we have encountered at least one woman who has problems with eating and body image. Although Leslie had already conquered the behavioral aspects of her anorexia, pregnancy, motherhood, and the changes in her body have called up old demons. Leslie's disclosures about herself reveal a new level of trust in the group. This also helps others to share some of the more difficult aspects of their own histories.

"Before Elyse, I had two miscarriages," says Ronnie. "That took a big toll on me, physically and emotionally. I was never sure if I could carry to term. This time when I got past the three-month mark and then the fourth and fifth months, it was an incredible joy. My body was finally working the way I hoped it would. It made this pregnancy seem so special, almost God-given. It also made me realize how out of my hands the whole thing is."

"I had an abortion when I was in my twenties," says Alicia. "All these years I've felt a little sad and guilty about it. And afraid, too, because I thought maybe it had damaged my body. Now I'm almost forty, but everything did what it was supposed to do. I was so relieved."

For women who have had miscarriages, abortions, or trouble conceiving, a successful pregnancy can be a longed-for end to disappointment and stress. As a prelude to the responsibilities of new motherhood, the nine months of pregnancy give all women time to come to terms with the changes in their bodies as well as the changes in their lives. The physical sensations of the quickening life inside help women to prepare for the upcoming work of childbirth.

⌒ LABOR AND CHILDBIRTH

Each individual woman knows her physical abilities and limits better than anyone else: how fast and long she can run, how much weight she can lift, how much sleep she needs, how she reacts to cold and heat, how she handles pain, hunger, thirst. Never before, however, has a woman been put to the test as she is by giving birth. Labor and childbirth are perhaps the most arduous physical tasks of a lifetime. Each woman's body, her pain threshold, the size and position of her baby, her physical and emotional preparation, and the medical and personal support she has, contribute to her experience.

Whether it is experienced as pain or as power, the physicality of bearing a child is undeniable. A woman feels and uses parts of her body she has never used before as her body performs this primary, physical function for the very first time. During labor a woman is a partner with her own body, following its course. She can neither hurry it along nor slow it down but works with it as it does its job.

The crescendo of contractions may last for six hours or twenty-six as it leads to the final hours of childbirth. Then comes the primal experience of forceful pushing, of sweating, of pain, of stretching and opening, of breathing and focus, possibly of vomiting and defecating, possibly of tearing or cutting, of bleeding, and finally of the triumph of delivery. Childbirth can be an exhilarating, sometimes frightening, always-powerful physical experience. Like war stories, birth stories must be told again and again.

"It was the most pain I've ever felt," Alicia begins. "I'm still having dreams about it. The breathing helped in the beginning, but I was doing those short pants you're supposed to save for the end when I got to three centimeters.

I had talked with my doctor about getting an epidural and I was already on the list for the anesthesiologist, but I had to wait my turn. That was the hardest part. I was moaning and thrashing about. I don't know how anyone can do it without drugs. The epidural was a godsend. It took away the unbearable pain, but I was still able to feel myself pushing. I was glad about that."

"I was afraid of childbirth," says Nan. "I've never been a very physical person. I don't exercise or jog or anything like that. But my doctor was great with me and I was stronger than I thought. I really surprised myself."

Changes in the practice of midwifery and obstetrics have been extensive in the past twenty years across the country. Expectant mothers participate far more in the birth process and natural childbirth is on the increase. Lamaze and Bradley classes have become part of the culture. Men learn to coach and support their partners and to help them cope with the pain of labor. Some women choose to deliver their babies at home. Many hospitals now offer alternative birthing centers for couples who wish to deliver their babies in a more homelike atmosphere without a lot of medical monitoring, but with doctors on hand in case they are needed. And most women, guided by their obstetricians or midwives, make their own decisions about the amount of drugs or painkillers they will use. However, if the birth they prepared for does not happen, many women blame themselves.

"I thought everything would go a certain way," Maggie says. "I had practiced my breathing. Done my Kegels every day. Hadn't gained too much weight. Didn't want any drugs. I was *prepared*. But after thirty hours of labor I wasn't progressing. I had to have an epidural and was given Pitosin to bring on labor more strongly. Then the baby's heart rate went down and it was like a house on fire. Bells went off. A dozen doctors in the room. It was as if I was no longer there. They cranked up my epidural and raced me down the hall to the operating room. I went from being completely involved to being numb from the neck down. My husband went from coaching to watching from the door window as they did an emergency C-section. I felt like I was watching a horror film. It was all so out there, not about me. Thank God, the baby was fine. It turned out he had a true knot in his cord. Even though everything turned out well, it took a long time for me to accept what happened."

Some twenty-five percent of births are cesarean sections. When the C-section is a medical emergency, it can be a tremendously stressful trial of both faith and mettle. Many women experience this as a kind of failure. They must recuperate not only from major surgery, but also from the upset of the often-traumatic experience of a surgical birth. It can be upsetting to have a firstborn ushered into the world while feeling frightenend and helpless. Especially when many women have experiences which they describe as empowering. Today more and more women share the experience of cesarean birth and gradually the onus of its being a failure is being shed. Additionally many women have planned C-sections which go smoothly, and these new mothers describe their experiences as positive. Some speak of a fast and easy recovery. Some speak of the pride they feel that, despite the obstacles, they were able to have a baby.

Most of the women in our groups agree that no matter what the details or circumstances, giving birth was the most dramatic event of their lives to date. There can be a thrilling sense of having performed a superhuman, yet quintessentially human, feat. While the pain usually dims in a woman's memory, the drama of childbirth will not. Mind and body have gone through an experience never to be forgotten.

～ POSTPARTUM

"For weeks after Lucy was born I felt like I had a pineapple between my legs," says Elizabeth. "I couldn't believe how long it took to feel better."

During the postpartum period a new mother's body is still going through change. She must cope with fluctuating hormones, a sore and swollen vagina and perineum, possible hemorrhoids, and some cramping and bleeding as her uterus contracts. Her body, now emptied of its baby, has yet another new shape and purpose.

Typically, three days after childbirth a new mother's milk will come in. When it does, her breasts may become rock hard as they fill and swell. If she made the decision to breast-feed, she is now, more than likely, consumed with mastering this new function of her body. It can take weeks before this process is going smoothly, before both mother and child feel capable and comfortable.

A woman's feelings about her breasts are psychologically loaded, weighted with feelings about her maturity, attractiveness, sexual identity, and sensuality. If she chooses to nurse her baby, her breasts also become linked to her feelings about herself as a mother, as a nurturer and soother. Breast feeding a baby is an intensely physical, intimate, and often sensual act. This too can change how a woman feels about her breasts in the sexual arena.

"The only reason I was unsure about breast feeding

was because I knew my breasts would get bigger," says Ronnie. "And I felt they were too big already. But I love to nurse Elyse. And now I know what my breasts are there for. It's pretty amazing to produce milk."

"I'm not used to having big breasts," says Leslie. "My husband likes my new body, but I find it almost embarrassing."

Jane laughs. "For me it's a bonus. I had aways wanted big breasts. Now I feel so womanly."

The postpartum term does not have a specific end date and yet the onset of menstruation after birth marks a return to a physical state of a more familiar and stable nature. There is a wide range to this timetable. For women who do not nurse, the menstrual cycle can begin anytime from six weeks to one year after birth. Women who breast-feed can get their period again anytime from three months to a year after the baby is born. Obstetricians and midwives remind new mothers that even if their periods have not started again, they may be fertile. Ovulation occurs before the first period returns. Birth control is required to prevent conception in postpartum women.

Many women report that their first periods are unusually heavy. In most cases this is a temporary change. Many women also report that they experience less frequent and less painful menstrual cramping. This is often a more lasting change.

ᢙᢙ GETTING BACK INTO YOUR CLOTHES

"It's been three months and I still can't get into any of my clothes. Thank goodness, the baby gets all the attention because I don't want people looking at me," says Ronnie.

"I was at the market the other evening without the baby," says Nan. "The woman next to me on line asked me when I was due. That did it. I'm really trying to lose weight now."

"I have been trying to be easy on myself and accept my body," says Jane. "I know I will eventually lose the weight. But the other night I found my husband looking at a Victoria's Secret catalogue and I suddenly felt so fat."

Although it is entirely normal, most women do not expect to have to wear larger sizes and even their maternity clothes three months into motherhood. Most women also do not expect hair loss, circles under the eyes, stretch marks, and extra padding. And a woman who had a C-section must now become acquainted with a scar on her belly. Altogether, a postpartum mother may feel as though she doesn't recognize herself. But this extra weight and padding are not meant to come off right away. It serves a purpose, providing the energy stores for nursing and a soft lap for a baby. When weight gain is slow and steady to come on, it is slow and steady to come off. We encourage new mothers to give themselves a full year to get back into shape.

Trying to work exercise into a new life as a mother can take months to figure out, especially since sleep is now hard to come by, and the energy may be lacking. In the early months, taking your baby for a daily stroll outside is good for both of you. Once your baby is sleeping longer at night, it can be a good time for a gradual return to more formal exercise. Exercise of any sort will give you increased energy, restored muscle tone, and a renewed sense of confidence in your body and yourself.

✑ POSTPARTUM DEPRESSION

"I've never cried so much in my life," says Jessica. "I thought this was supposed to be a happy time."

At the mercy of changing hormone levels and fatigue, most new mothers cry a lot. After giving birth, the body undergoes a normal and rapid drop of estrogen. This can cause hot flashes, depressive symptoms, and difficulty with concentration. During the first weeks and early months of your baby's life, and of your life as a mother, your emotions will be strongly felt, sometimes soaring, sometimes raw and bitter. Most new mothers encounter a sense of sadness as they adjust to their new roles. Seven to ten percent of new mothers experience postpartum depression.

Crying is normal for all new mothers. Periods of depression are also common. But it may be hard for a new mother to label herself as depressed because she is experiencing such a range of emotional responses to her new role. And because she *is* affected by isolation, stress, and lack of sleep, many of her feelings are to be expected. They may include panic about the responsibilities of parenthood and about the health of her new baby, doubts about her maternal feelings toward her newborn, and a form of grief at the loss of her former life.

But when bouts of inexplicable weepiness turn into continual feelings of melancholy, when sadness or anxiety begins to interfere with your ability to care for your baby and yourself, then it is probably time to seek the help of a medical or mental health professional. Talk to your obstetrician or internist about your depression. Or, if there is a program or clinic for new mothers at your local hospital, ask there for advice. Counseling, support groups, and antidepressant medications are avenues to explore which can be of help.

Having a baby is seen by the world as a gain rather than a loss. So the new mother who feels any sense of loss will commonly keep it to herself, another secret shame. In truth, though, she has experienced some rather fundamental losses—a loss of her former life, of the stability she once had, of the body and identity she always had. Some degree of depression can be seen as a healthy and natural reaction to these radical changes.

As new mothers responsible for introducing the idea of a healthy body image in your children, you need to recognize and defend yourselves against the pervasive societal pressure to be thin. You need to strive actively to overcome self-critical feelings and to be gentle with yourself. You are now a model for your children. How you feel about and express yourself regarding your body will strongly influence your children's body sense. Feeling good about yourself will help to instill a positive body image and a strong sense of pride and self-acceptance in your children.

Mothering is intensely physical. As a mother-to-be, your body is creator, incubator, provider, and protector. As a mother, your body makes milk, provides warmth, and security. You feed your baby, rock and carry her, and cradle her in your arms. She knows your smell. She roots for milk. She falls asleep next to you. More than anyone else ever can, she needs your body. She loves and appreciates your body. So should you.

SIX

Rock-A-Bye Baby
The Importance of Sleep

"I thought sleep would come to my baby," says Maggie. "I thought that one night I would put Jack in his crib and he would sleep all night long."

Like many first-time mothers, Maggie had no idea that getting her baby to sleep on his own would take some doing. She was prepared to be up at night to feed and pace with her newborn for the first two months or so but expected that Jack would eventually learn to sleep by himself, as naturally as he would one day learn to sit up.

And, in fact, it seemed that Jack was on that route. At thirteen weeks, he had settled into a pattern of going to sleep at 10:30 P.M. and waking up only once in the night. At fourteen weeks he had slept through the night from 10:30 P.M. until 6:30 A.M. Maggie and Tom were pleased and relieved to finally get back into a rhythm of uninterrupted sleep themselves. But then, when he was fifteen weeks old, Jack began to protest at bedtime and to wake up again at night. He woke up three, then four and then five times. He required extra long periods of rocking,

141

nursing, and soothing to get back to sleep. After three nights of this, Maggie and Tom began to worry that there was something wrong with Jack, that he was sick or in some sort of discomfort. Maggie spoke with the pediatrician on the telephone. The doctor told her he was not alarmed but agreed to schedule an appointment for the following day. As the pediatrician had suspected, there was nothing medically wrong with Jack. He told Maggie that this change was not atypical and that Jack, at fifteen and a half weeks and fourteen pounds, was capable of sleeping through the night as he had already demonstrated the week before. He suggested that Maggie and Tom would have to tolerate Jack's crying in order for him to learn to fall to sleep on his own. Maggie was anxious to discuss Jack's sleep further in the next mother-infant group, which was two days off.

In the meantime, Maggie pored through the literature on babies and sleep. She found that one expert advocated letting the baby cry it out; another believed in responding to the baby's every cry; one suggested a warm bath before bed; one believed in the family bed. Maggie found one approach almost too clinical, and another too general to help. Maggie started to give Jack formula at night, an option the pediatrician had suggested. Jack took easily to the formula but it had no effect on his night wakings, which continued to shatter the family's sleep.

You may have noticed a change in your baby's sleep habits, as Maggie did. His night wakings may have decreased and then suddenly increased for no apparent reason and settling your baby down to sleep may have started to take longer and longer. Even if you have rocked him to sleep in your arms, the moment you put him in the crib his eyes open, his head pops up, and the roaring protest begins.

"Please, please, please, please go to sleep," you catch yourself begging.

Unwilling to tolerate his cries, you try again to rock him to sleep. After twenty minutes, his body relaxes in your arms and you carefully lower him into his crib, holding your breath all the while. It works. Bliss. But these nights you can only count on a couple of hours of sleep, if you can fall asleep at all.

As your baby's nocturnal demands increase and your hours of sleep decrease, life becomes fuzzy around the edges. Everyone you speak to may have a different opinion. You may begin to think that this is your lot in life. As the days go by you are less productive, less able to cope. Then, burning frustration and even anger can set in. Sleep deprived, you struggle with the simplest of tasks, bristle when your spouse says that things have got to change, and snap like a twig when your mother suggests letting the baby cry it out.

This is when we meet many of the parents we counsel outside of our groups. Exhausted, befuddled, disheartened, they feel they have done something to bring this upon themselves. Often couples are embroiled in conflict with one another about how to proceed. Lack of sleep has brought out the worst in them, they confess, and it has begun to make them resent each other and their own child. What, they ask, can they do? There are many schools of thought about babies and sleep. As Maggie discovered, the literature *can* feel like a maze of options. How and when to respond to a baby who cries in the night has become an area of some controversy even among the experts.

It is clear to us that there can be no single plan to get a baby to sleep at night that works for all families. All babies are not the same in their sleep habits and even the same baby will be different in his sleep habits at different ages. Parents have different goals and tolerances for their babies' sleep habits. And each man and woman brings his and her own unique emotional history to the job of helping their baby learn to sleep. Our thinking regarding babies and sleep has been most influenced by the work of Dr. Richard Ferber, pediatrician, director of the Center for Pediatric Sleep Disorders at Children's Hospital in Boston, and author of *Solve Your Child's Sleep Problems.* (Simon & Schuster, New York, 1985). Our approach has been shaped by nearly a decade of clinical experience with new mothers in group settings, by individual work with couples who come to us specifically for sleep counseling for their babies, and by our personal and individual experiences with our own children. Each of these has helped us to understand how critically important it is to the whole family for a baby to sleep well, how necessary it is for a baby to consistently get enough hours of sleep, and how difficult it can be for parents to help their babies do so. If you are having trouble with your baby's sleep, you are in good company. Most parents struggle with this. It is our goal to help you understand and minimize some of the upheaval, confusion, and anxiety that can accompany the process of helping your baby learn to sleep through the night.

It is a cold and overcast day in mid December. Wind sweeps down the avenues and the forecast speaks of an early snow. As the women arrive, they greet each other enthusiastically. They cluster in small groups, exchanging stories and admiring each others' babies. Alicia asks Jane to watch Keith while she gets some coffee. Elizabeth helps Ronnie get Elyse out of her sling. Leslie's baby, Eric, sat up this week, she announces, and there is a round of applause.

The atmosphere in the room is easy and collegial. Sometimes it has the feeling of a club, a place for new-mothers-only. The women are comfortable and open with one another. Everyone gets a chance to speak and to ask questions. Those who are brimming with concern usually go first.

"I'm obsessed with Elyse's sleep," says Ronnie. "When should her bedtime be? Should I still be nursing her to sleep? Should I let her nap in the swing? My husband and I are beginning to argue about all of this. It's crazy."

The mothers agree that their babies' sleep is a consuming preoccupation. Alicia is upset because she and her nanny are at odds over Keith's bedtime. Leslie tells us that she and her husband are fighting about when or if to respond to Eric's cries at night. Both Maggie and Marta agree that the issue of sleep is the most provocative part of parenting for them.

Sleep is the developmental topic that receives the most extensive focus in our eight-part mother-infant group meetings. Our group discussion on this issue is never limited to one meeting. Sleep is an ongoing topic of concern and interest brought up by one or the other of the mothers each week.

✎ ROCK-A-BYE BABY: 0–3 MONTHS

The sleep patterns of a newborn are unpredictable. And during their first weeks there is no typical behavior. Some newborns will sleep the better part of their first two weeks, occasionally waking to feed and blink at the world before going back to sleep. Other newborns arrive wide-eyed, rarely sleeping for longer than an hour at a time. Almost all newborns will wake crying to be fed two or three times in the night and sometimes more. It is during these first weeks that parents learn what it takes to get their baby to fall asleep.

Justin is seventeen weeks old. He needs constant movement in order to fall asleep. Jane says she has rocked Justin's bassinette so much the rug beneath it has become worn. "It may be a bad habit," Jane admits, "but it's the only one that stops him from crying and gets him to sleep."

Elizabeth's baby, Lucy, is now sixteen weeks old. "Lucy usually falls asleep when she is nursing," says Elizabeth. "When I was interviewing day-care people, I thought what I really needed was a wet nurse."

Nan's baby, Emma, has a strong need to suck. For her naps, Nan puts half a dozen pacifiers in Emma's bassinette so that she'll never be far from one. Jessica takes Nell for nightly drives up pothole-ridden First Avenue and finds that the combination of gray noise and bumpy motion helps.

A baby's first three months can be thought of as his fourth trimester, a time of transition from the womb to the world. After nine months inside of his mother, a baby is accustomed to being gently rocked, continuously fed, warm, dark, and always close to the sound of his mother's voice and heartbeat. There everything was regulated for him, but now, out in a bright, new environment, he is totally dependent on your help. To get to sleep your baby may need to be swaddled and held, jiggled and walked, fed and rocked. You need not worry about setting up "bad habits" during these first three months. Some mothers swear by the automatic swing, others by the Snugli, some stroll their babies to get them to nod off, some bounce and dance and pat their babies to sleep. You can feel proud of whatever method you devise that works.

Your options for where your baby will sleep are also wide-open during these early months. He can sleep in a bassinette, a basket, a crib, or in bed with you. He can sleep in your bedroom, in the hallway nearby, or in a separate bedroom. In part, your decision depends on the nature of your own sleep—whether you are awakened by your baby's every toss or cough, whether you can fall back to sleep easily having been awakened by his normal stirrings, or whether you sleep best when your baby is right at hand. Your baby's needs, as well as your own, are part of this decision.

"Most nights Emma sleeps in bed with us," says Nan. "It works well. She sleeps wonderfully. I don't have to get out of bed for the middle-of-the-night nursing and Rick feels included. I don't think this will go on forever, but I do love having her right next to me at night."

For now, sharing a bed is the most natural arrangement for Nan's family. As long as it is working for everyone it is an intimate and effective way of easing Emma into the world. During the day Emma is capable of sleeping without her mother's body next to her, napping in a bassinet in her parents' bedroom. Eventually, Nan wants Emma to sleep in her own room, as does Rick. But Nan is not yet ready for that kind of separation from her baby.

"Sarah slept in my bed every night for almost two months after I got her," says Marta. "I think it was important for both of us to be close like that. I wanted her to physically know who I was and to know that I was there for her, that I would be her mother. But then she learned to flip over and I was too nervous about her falling out of bed to fall asleep myself. So I started putting her in her crib at bedtime. Sometimes I'll bring her back to my bed after her bottle in the middle of the night."

No matter how you get your baby to sleep, or where he sleeps, there are ways to set the stage for good sleep patterns during these first three months. A first step is to help your baby learn that night and daytime sleep are different. During the day your baby may snooze in a stroller, car seat, Snugli or in his crib. But at night, anytime after about nine o'clock, it's a good idea to put your baby to sleep in the crib where he will be for the night. To further distinguish night sleep from day sleep, feedings in the middle of the night should be done in semidarkness. Although he is irresistible, try not to engage your baby in a way which will make him come even more awake. This can be an intimate time for parent and child, but it should not be a social one.

"When I hear Elyse cry out in the middle of the night I get a thrill," says Ronnie. "I may be cross-eyed tired, but I'm excited at the same time. It's sort of the way I felt as a child on the night before my birthday. I can't believe I have a baby! Then, as I'm rocking Elyse back to sleep, a deep fatigue hits me and all I want in the world is a full night of sleep."

You *will* be especially tired during the first three months of motherhood. Broken and insufficient sleep are hallmarks of this period. Some mothers become chronically overtired. Some babies can, too. If you have tried for a long time to soothe your crying baby and feel unable to continue trying, you can put him in his crib for five or ten minutes. Some babies will cry for a little while but then quickly fall asleep. In this case, crying may be his way to block out stimulation. If your baby does not stop crying within ten minutes, you should go to him. While it will not harm him, a baby will not benefit in any way from extensive crying at this early age.

It takes tremendous energy and commitment to respond to a new baby's needs and learn how best to soothe him. It requires endurance to exist on limited hours of sleep at night. But this early phase does not go on forever. Your baby will soon be able to sleep for much longer stretches. And so will you.

ᥱᢐ THE TRANSITION PHASE: 3–4 MONTHS

Some time around the three-month mark babies start to sleep longer at night. They also begin to be able to wait for longer periods between feedings. They cry less, are increasingly interested in you and the world around them, and begin to interact and vocalize more. These changes are evidence of dramatic cognitive development in your baby. As you see these changes you will know the time is right to begin to take over the controls and to lay the foundations for a new sleep schedule for your baby.

Babies thrive on regular routines and can learn to anticipate them. A bedtime routine every evening is an easy way to start to teach your baby about sleeping through the night. Soon your baby will recognize this special routine as a signal that bedtime is at hand. If a warm bath tends to calm and quiet your baby, it can be a good idea to start his routine with an evening bath. Infant daytime clothes are not very different from their nighttime clothes, but changing your baby into pajamas is something he will also learn to associate with bedtime.

You can come up with any calming "good-night" routine you like and it can last from fifteen to forty-five minutes. The idea is to help your baby gradually unwind, relax, and prepare for the separation that is sleep. Once your baby is in his bed clothes, read him a bedtime story, sing him a soothing song, or gently rock him to a lullaby tape. Babies often need an extra dose of physical contact before they are willing to let go for the night. For the first three months many mothers nurse or bottle-feed their babies to sleep. After three months, you can continue to include feeding as part of the bedtime routine. But starting now, you can begin to experiment with your baby's capacity for doing the last bit of falling asleep on his own. Ultimately, your goal will be to put your baby in his crib *before* he has fallen asleep in your arms and to let him learn that he can do this by himself.

When he was fifteen weeks old Jack exhibited the classic signs that his sleep patterns were in transition: they improved for a short while, then dramatically worsened. Having struggled for over a week, Maggie is anxious to talk. We listen to her description of her week, then ask her to lay out Jack's sleep schedule for us in detail.

"Jack wakes up at 6:00 A.M. He takes two two-hour naps a day and goes to sleep between ten-thirty and eleven at night. He is alert and happy during the day. But the time between six and nine at night I call the 'Hell Hours.' He becomes like a different baby. I think he might have gas or colic. On the evenings that Tom is home, he can't believe Jack is so fussy. We have to pace with him forever, but he doesn't get sleepy like he used to."

Another change that happens at the three-to-four-month mark is that babies become able to keep themselves awake. They are increasingly interested in the world, they are intensely interested in you and can actively fight sleep. Maggie has been waiting for a sign that Jack is tired, but the opportune time to put a baby to bed is *before* he acts tired. Once a baby shows you that he is tired, he is *overtired*. He may have gotten a second wind. He may seem alert but be quick to tears. As it gets later and later he becomes exhausted and has even greater difficulty falling asleep.

There is a certain beauty to the timing of sleep problems at the three-to-four-month stage. Directly following the age when babies become capable of sleeping longer and seem to be headed in that direction, they often will do this kind of an about-face. Their steadily improving sleep patterns suddenly worsen. And then a baby will dramatically digress, waking more frequently and protesting more strongly at bedtime. These can be seen as signals that your baby needs your help in regulating his sleep *and* that he is ready for it.

Even though Jack has been going to bed at ten-thirty or eleven o'clock at night for three months, his cranky evening hours are a cue that he is now ready for an earlier bedtime. We recommend a 7:30 or 8:00 P.M. bedtime for healthy babies between three and four months old. The switch to this earlier bedtime can be made either gradually or all at once.

"Are you listening, Nellie?" Jessica asks her daughter.

"Some babies may be able to go to bed that early," Nan protests, "but not Emma. I know her."

Often the hardest person to convince of the feasibility of a 7:30 bedtime is the parent. We ask the mothers to think about it, to talk about it, to watch their babies for evening crankiness, worsening sleeping patterns, and other signs of change.

Alicia groans and says, "I knew the nanny was right but I'll never see Keith if he goes to bed at seven-thirty."

This is a real bind for Alicia and other working parents who get home late. The 7:30 bedtime is optimal for the baby, but it is more important for parents and their babies to have a chance to be together. If your work schedule cannot be changed, set your baby's bedtime later than 7:30 or 8:00 P.M. Continue, however, to treat these hours as winding-down time.

Maggie is still upset. "Now you're saying seven-thirty is optimal but I can't get Jack to bed period. How can I expect him to start sleeping twelve hours a night when up until now he's been sleeping only eight?"

This leads us to a deceptively simple and exceptionally golden rule: Sleep begets sleep. The longer your baby sleeps, the more he will sleep. The more regular and scheduled your baby's sleep becomes, the more sleep he will take. You can count on this. He will thrive on it.

～ SLEEPING THROUGH THE NIGHT: 4–12 MONTHS

By the time they are four months old, babies need eleven to twelve hours of uninterrupted sleep at night and two naps a day of at least one hour each. They need this amount of sleep in order to develop optimally. What surprises most parents is the invariability of this developmental fact: at this age, all babies do best with fourteen hours or more of sleep during the course of a twenty-four-hour period.

When your baby is cranky or miserable because of insufficient sleep, it is easy to see the importance of regulating his sleep. But if your baby is not overtly overtired on fewer hours of sleep, you may not be convinced that fourteen sleeping hours a day is necessary for him. Many mothers, in fact, have said their babies seem fine on nine or ten hours of sleep. But once these babies started to get thirteen or fourteen hours a day, their mothers reported positive changes as well. Their babies became happier, more social, more focused, more open to learning and play.

"You're telling me I'll be putting Elyse to bed at seven-thirty and she won't nurse again until morning? She'll starve! She'll never be able to do it," Ronnie insists, adding, as she holds her breasts, "I'll never be able to do it either."

If your baby is four months old, was born at full term, is healthy, and weighs at least twelve pounds, he is capable of sleeping through the night for eleven to twelve hours without a feeding. This does not depend on whether he is breast-fed, formula-fed, or has begun to eat cereal. At this age babies are physically able to give up their nighttime feedings and will naturally eat more during the day to meet their nutritional needs. Because it activates the digestive system, a feeding in the middle of the night can actually be disruptive to sleep. By not feeding your baby in the middle of the night, his metabolism is allowed to slow down, which, in turn, promotes sleep.

Babies, like adults, go through cycles of deep sleep, light sleep, and brief wakings throughout the night. Most adults hardly notice these shifts and generally get through a night without disruption. Babies, however, need to learn how to fall asleep and how to get back to sleep on their own after these normal, intermittent night wakings.

By four months babies also have an increased capacity for memory and can learn from repeated experiences. While he did not come into the world knowing how to settle himself to sleep, he is now capable of learning. The teaching is easier before a baby makes fixed associations to how he goes to sleep and before he learns to sit, crawl, or pull himself to standing.

Imagine this: In two weeks time your four-and-a-half-month-old baby goes to bed at seven-thirty with hardly a fuss and sleeps through the night until six-thirty in the morning. During the day he naps from nine until ten in the morning and from two until three-thirty in the afternoon. He is generally alert and happy and rarely cranky. You probably can't believe it, but this is a realistic goal and one that parents have helped their babies to realize again and again.

Now imagine this: Years of nighttimes dominated by your baby's bad sleep habits. The horror stories we've heard are plentiful. Here are a sampling:

A two-and-a-half-year-old girl has been waking up two and three times a night almost every night since she was four months old. Her parents tried sleep training but were unable to stick with it long enough to make it work, and then resigned themselves to nights of broken sleep. The child is chronically overtired and now, the mother, who is pregnant with their second child, needs her sleep more than ever.

A three-year-old boy will not fall asleep without his mother rubbing his back as she has always done. This takes thirty to forty-five minutes at bedtime and often once in the middle of the night. Sometimes at two or three in the morning the boy will climb into his parents' bed, at which time they are too tired to resist and let him stay. Embarrassed to ask a baby-sitter to go through any part of this ritual, the parents have stopped going out at night.

A four-year-old is so overtired during the daytime that he is unable to participate happily in group activities. Yet he refuses to go to bed at night. When his parents try to make him, the boy gets so upset that he throws up. At his mercy, the parents let him watch videos until he falls asleep on the couch, sometimes at 11:00 P.M., sometimes later, and then carry him to his bed.

The stories are endless. And oftentimes the essential, and only, reason a baby will not learn good sleep habits is because a parent cannot bear to hear him cry.

ᗌᗢ CRYING

In all likelihood your baby came into this world crying. To you it meant your baby was alive and well and you, too, may have wept, with pleasure and relief, at the sound. By now you've learned to recognize the subtle differences in your baby's cries and the different messages they convey. "Oh, that's a hungry cry," you say and look at your watch to see how long it has been since his last feeding. "That's a bored cry," you explain as he fusses in his car seat. It can be a guessing game. Maybe he needs a new diaper or maybe he has gas. Or, it can be obvious. A loud noise, a sudden light, a fast movement has frightened your baby. His mouth opens wide into a silent scream, he catches his breath and then cries out. If your baby had colic, you know the inconsolable cry of a baby in pain. Even if your baby does not have colic, you are probably aware of a point in every day when he cries for no apparent reason. It may be late afternoon or early evening, mirroring the fatigue of the whole family.

On the first night of helping your baby learn to sleep through the night you will hear a new theme in his repertoire of crying songs: that of protest and rage. When you do not respond right away to your baby's cries he will become angry and then even enraged. It can be almost frightening to hear this new kind of cry and this intense emotion from your little baby, to hear it grow and grow, and to know that you have allowed it. To be rational in the face of a baby's outrage is very difficult. To proceed with your plan can seem impossible.

"Do we have to do the crying thing? Isn't there any way around it?" Jane asks.

Listening to your baby cry, if only for ten minutes at a stretch, can be gut-wrenching. It can weaken the resolve of anyone but the most determined or the most desperate. But, unfortunately, it is almost always necessary to endure some crying in order to help your baby learn to soothe himself, fall asleep on his own, and sleep through the night. We hope to help you untangle your emotions from your baby's needs during this critical time. We hope to help you to keep your goals and your baby's best interests in sight.

We've known babies who have learned to sleep through the night after a few episodes of crying during one night. We've also known babies who took well over two weeks to learn this skill. Much depends on your baby's personality, but the older a baby is when you start, the more time the process may take. You can safely start when your baby is three to four months old and weighs twelve pounds. At four months a baby may need only two nights to get on track. At ten months, a baby may take a week or ten days. These ten days may feel like the longest days of your life.

Marta lets out a sigh. She is obviously upset as she describes Sarah's sleep patterns.

"I thought things were going pretty well with Sarah's sleep. It wasn't easy, but it was manageable. Then we went to my sister's for Thanksgiving and stayed for the weekend. My sister couldn't believe I was still getting up at night two and three times. Since we've been home things have been getting even worse. Sarah's waking almost every two hours now. I can get her back to sleep if I feed her or bring her into my bed. But I'm upset about going back to so many bottles at night. I've always heard it was supposed to get easier at three months, not harder. I don't know what to do anymore. What's wrong?"

Having regularly worked with mothers at this especially confusing juncture, it is easy to hear the confusion and guilt in Marta's question. She may as well have asked, "What have I done wrong?" Usually there is no single wrong to right, no single switch to flip. In Marta's case there are a number of things to consider regarding her feelings of guilt. First is the very common instinct a new mother has to continue doing what she has always done to soothe her baby to sleep despite the fact that her baby is changing. At fifteen weeks, Sarah is exactly in the middle of the transition phase. She is ready for a consistent sleep routine. Next is the holiday disruption of Sarah's schedule. Any overnight trip can throw a baby for a loop and it can take several days to get back to normal. This is no reason to avoid travel, but it is the price one pays. Last is Marta's sister's response, which made Marta wonder if she should be getting up at night for Sarah at all.

Marta goes on. "I know you said I couldn't spoil her at this age, but maybe I *have* made her too dependent on me. I never let her cry. I never want to let her cry. I can't imagine doing this sleep training. I get tense even thinking about it. If I let her cry, she'd think I don't care. She would feel unhappy and lonely. Eventually she would feel deserted!"

Marta is quiet and the group waits for her to continue. After a pause, Marta says, "I've messed up, haven't I? I didn't want rules for my baby. I wanted to be different. More flexible and giving. My mother and father were so strict with me, so removed."

Marta's need to be superresponsive to her baby is fueled in part by old hurt. During the early months of motherhood, Marta's ability to soothe and protect her baby fulfilled a deep need for Marta. But as Marta realizes that Sarah's interrupted night sleep is not good for her, she becomes torn and upset. She feels the need to set limits but cannot tolerate even the idea of Sarah crying. Setting limits has become confused with being punitive and distant. Making this connection and putting her feelings into a larger context help Marta to rethink her plans.

Most parents attribute all sorts of negative, adult emotions to the cries of their infant children. Referred to as projection, this very common reaction can be an effective stumbling block to helping a baby learn to fall asleep on his own. When we ask the rest of the mothers to imagine how their babies would feel if left to cry for a period of five minutes, their answers come fast and furious.

"She would feel abandoned." "He would be scared!" "He would panic at the idea of not being fed." "She would wonder where the hell I was." "He would feel lost, helpless." "She would be afraid of the dark."

The sound of your baby crying can evoke powerful, raw emotions. Some parents describe it as merely unpleasant, while others say it is physically painful for them. Listening to your baby cry can stir feelings from childhood. You may remember being afraid of monsters or of the dark. But there is a big difference in the memories of fright of older children and what is going on in an infant's mind. When your baby cries, he is not scared. He is not thinking of monsters or of the dark. He most probably is frustrated, upset, and angry. Because he cannot talk, he cries. Some parents tell us that it helps them to understand these cries as those of frustration and anger rather than of fear or sadness. Your baby was dependent on your help to get to sleep. He was accustomed to being fed, rocked, and sung to at any hour of the night. And now you are setting his very first and earliest limit. He is just plain angry. And no wonder.

Children of any age will protest against limits. Ultimately, however, they need limits, feel safe and protected by them. When a parent sets limits on candy or television with a two-year-old, for instance, the child's tantrum is considered normal and benign, not at all pleasant, but almost to be expected at this age. So, when you set a limit regarding sleep with your five-month-old baby, try to think of his crying spell as a normal response to this limit. Letting your baby cry at night for a controlled period of time and for the purpose of regulating his sleep will not harm him nor damage your relationship with him. He will still love you in the morning.

∽ WHEN SPOUSES DISAGREE

Another potential stumbling block to teaching a baby how to sleep through the night is conflict between husband and wife. Often couples are at bitter odds over how to deal with their baby's crying. Disagreements blister in the night, especially when the crying triggers different emotions in each partner. Unfortunately, arguments about a baby's sleep patterns can become an outlet for resentment that has built up between couples over other issues.

Leslie has been fighting with Vince about letting five-month-old Eric cry at night.

"Vince has a really hard time listening to Eric cry. It just kills him. He goes nuts after about three minutes. I think Eric is ready to stop nursing at night. So, when he cries at two in the morning I give him his pacifier, or rub his tummy. But I try not to nurse him. Then I put him in his crib . . . and pray. Sometimes he'll settle down but if he doesn't, Vince insists that I give in. And, inevitably, I nurse him to sleep. Sometimes it takes as little as a minute of nursing before Eric's asleep, so I know it's not that he's hungry.

"Vince thinks the baby is too young to be left to cry. I think the baby is too old to still be needing me every night. I don't like to hear him cry either, but I think I have the right to get him to sleep through the night. After all, I'm the one who is taking care of him all day. I think I know what's right here."

The differences in attitudes, vulnerabilities, and expectations between Leslie and Vince have come to a head. Meanwhile, their inconsistent messages to Eric—of letting him cry and then responding, of letting him cry again and then nursing him—have made Eric confused and increasingly demanding.

Leslie continues. "When a baby is breast-fed, I think the father feels powerless. That's what we were fighting about last night. Vince was threatening to give Eric a bottle if I wouldn't nurse him. It got into a huge contest of wills. I lost. And now I don't see how anything is going to change."

Leslie and Vince need to set aside some time to talk without drama or interruption during the calm of day instead of over the baby's head in the dead of night. It will be important for each of them to agree to disengage from battle in order to explore their feelings about teaching Eric to sleep. It can be helpful if a husband and wife try to figure out what their baby's cries are triggering in each of them.

The following week, Leslie tells us that she and Vince went out for coffee and that, in the setting of a public place, they were able to talk together much more thoughtfully and sensitively. Vince told Leslie that he resented being left out of each and every decision about their baby. He said he didn't understand how Leslie could be so unemotional about Eric's crying. Leslie admitted that she had been bull-headed in the way she had assumed the right to make all the decisions but felt in need of control in her job as mother.

"Maybe it's because I was fired from my job," Leslie says. "That was so awful. I'm not really over it. But all of Vince's opinions just sound like criticism, like I'm not doing this job right either. He's so overbearing."

During their talk, Vince tried to get at why Eric's cries make him feel anxious. As the fourth of five children, Vince says he rarely got enough of his parents' undivided attention when he was growing up. He doesn't want Eric to have to experience that feeling. Leslie, on the other hand, tells the group that much of her growing up was spent trying to become independent of her parents. Her parents were very involved in her life, and in some ways their high expectations for her made her want to run. She wants to give Eric space to work things out on his own.

If one partner cannot tolerate the baby's cries and is very emotional about it, the other partner will often take on the role of "the reasonable one." Vince's response to Eric's cries are clearly tied to his feelings from childhood. Leslie's nonresponse may appear to be the rational one, but it, too, is an emotional response. It is helpful to remember that there is no good guy or bad guy in this process. Both parents' feelings and opinions play an important part. Leslie and Vince had been fighting about Eric's sleep but it wasn't sleep that was at issue. Their feelings of resentment, powerlessness, and old hurt were blocking any chance of coming to an agreement about Eric. Having made a breakthrough in communication that led to a better understanding of what Eric's cries elicit in each of them, they will be more effective supporting one another.

If you try to work together through this provocative period, it can help you to feel closer as a couple. Ideally you will be able to proceed as a team, focusing on your baby's needs as well as your own. Once your baby starts sleeping more regularly, life will resume more normal patterns. You and your spouse will have more time for yourselves and for each other.

∿ THE HOW-TOS

You and your husband have decided that you are ready— or desperate enough—to try to teach your baby good sleeping habits. After endless nights of broken sleep, a new logic has emerged: This is not good for our baby. Or for us. So now what?

- *Enlist each other's support.* Sleep work is best when both parents are actively involved. If you are a single parent, or if your spouse is regularly away on business, ask a friend to help you. This could be your sister, your mother, anyone who knows both you and your baby well and who would be willing to spend the night at your house and go through the process with you. It should be someone with whom you can talk openly about your feelings and plans, someone you can lean on for support and encouragement when you are faltering.

- *Clarify your motivations.* Write down your goals and the reasons behind them. Include words of wisdom to yourself because you may well be turning for reassurance to these ideas at a weak moment in the middle of the night. For example, you might write:

  We can't go on like this. The baby is always cranky. I am overtired. My husband and I are fighting.

  The baby could be waking up every night like this until he is two or three years old.

  Other babies sleep well. So can ours.

  This is in our baby's best interests.

- *Select a day to start.* A Friday or Saturday night is a good choice because you will not have the pressure of a workday hanging over you. Don't make other plans for the evenings during the first week of sleep work. Make your baby's sleep training your only commitment.

- *Set your waiting interval.* Choose an amount of time that you think you could tolerate listening to your baby cry without going to him and without feeling pushed over the edge yourself. Whatever you decide, this will be the period to wait before you go to check on your baby the first time. Keep in mind that babies need time to work through their crying and to figure out some self-soothing techniques. We think five minutes is the minimum amount a baby can make use of effectively. The whole process will go more quickly if this interval is longer. If you think you can handle it, set your first waiting interval at ten or fifteen minutes.

- *Put your baby in his crib before he is asleep.* On the first night at seven-thirty or eight, it's bedtime as usual. Use your baby's now-familiar bedtime routine to ready him for the night. Carefully watch your baby to be sure he does not fall asleep in your arms or at your breast. Put him in his crib when he is drowsy but not fully asleep. Even if your baby does not appear tired, put him in his crib. Say goodnight in a loving manner. Try to rid your voice of guilt or pleading. Your baby will better understand that you mean business from a convinced tone of voice. So try to sound like you mean it. Then leave the room.

- *Look at the clock when your baby begins to cry.* Make a note of the time your baby wakes up and keep track of the duration of his cries. It can be helpful to have this to hold on to in the middle of the night so you can see your baby's progress, however slight.

- *Time your first waiting interval.* If this is the first time you have put your baby in his crib before he is asleep, he will probably cry right away and the first timed interval of his crying and your waiting will begin right then, at the bedtime hour. Sometimes a baby will awaken forty minutes to an hour after he has fallen asleep at bedtime and parents can misread this short sleep as an early evening nap. However, no matter when the first waking occurs, treat it as a night waking, not as a nap. If your baby is at the stage where he can drift off to sleep on his own, then the first timed interval will begin when he awakens later in the night.

- *Support one another.* If it is the middle of the night and one of you is still sleeping, rouse your partner. Both of you should be fully awake so that you can support each other during the timed waiting interval before you check on your baby. If either of you feels yourself faltering, remind each other of your goals. Read over your motivation sheet. Remember that this is short-term and well worth the effort.

- *Listen to your baby cry.* Parents respond differently to this difficult task. You may decide you need to listen intently to every cry and gasp your baby makes. If so, it may help you to make something of an exercise of this. You can try to discern the rhythm to your baby's cries as it changes in intensity and timbre; you can try to identify the moment when your baby switches from angry cries to an accepting cry as he begins to soothe himself. Alternatively, you may decide that you need some emotional distance from your baby's crying. It may help you to listen from farther away, to focus only on the passing minutes, or to avoid listening altogether. (Although one partner should listen at all times.) If the sound of your baby crying becomes too painful for either of you, have that person take a break: take a walk, a shower, or listen to music on headphones.

Make it a point to try to understand what the crying elicits in you. Is it fear? Is it anxiety? Discerning your own response can shed light on how you project your past onto your baby's cries. It may help you to go forward.

- *Check in.* After you have waited for your set amount of time, check on your baby. Either parent can do this, but if you are doing sleep training with a friend, check-ins are best done by the child's parent. Checking in serves two purposes. One is to reassure your baby that you are still there. The other is to reassure you that, although clearly upset, your baby is in no danger. When you check on your baby, keep it short—no longer than one to two minutes. Leave the lights off. Don't feed your baby. This is not meant to be a time to soothe your baby back to sleep the way you always have, but you can gently fix his blanket, pat his head, rub his back or stomach, find his pacifier for him, and say some soothing words. Some parents develop a routine of rhythmic back-patting and "shhhh"-chanting. We don't usually recommend that you pick your baby up, but you can try it to see his response. It may help him break the cycle of crying and give him a fresh start; if so, great. On the other hand it may confuse and frustrate your baby when you put him back to bed. In general, we have found it works best to do the least amount you can before leaving the room.

Of course, when your baby is upset your natural inclination will be to soothe him, to pick him up and rock him. But during this process of sleep work you will have to resist these instincts. Going against the desire to soothe your baby as you always have is one of the most difficult parts of sleep work for all new parents.

- *Extend your timed waiting interval.* After the first check-in, extend the amount of time you wait before the next check-in. You can increase by single minutes or by five minutes depending on how much you think you can handle. For example: ten minutes of crying. Check in. Fifteen minutes of crying. Check in. Twenty minutes of crying. Check in. Once you have doubled the waiting time you started with, keep checking in at this new interval until your baby falls asleep. Frequent check-ins can interrupt a baby's process of settling down. By doubling your initial timed waiting interval, you give your baby more of a chance to learn to soothe himself.

- *Time your second waiting interval.* If there is a pause in your baby's cries and then he resumes, begin timing anew. Your baby will most likely continue to cry after you have checked in on him, so look at the clock again; note the end of your first check-in time and the beginning of the second waiting interval. Then prepare to wait again while your baby cries.

- *Be consistent.* Although many families falter a few times during sleep training, try to remember that if you do give in and feed or rock your baby to sleep after a prolonged interval of crying, his crying has been for naught. Your baby has not learned that he is capable of falling asleep on his own. He has not learned to soothe himself. He has only learned that unrelenting crying will eventually bring you to him. Hold on to this idea when your resolve feels low. Whatever amount of waiting time you have chosen, talk your plan through with your partner. And help each other to be consistent. The payoff for you and your baby is within sight.

∿ "BUT, WHAT IF . . . ?"

Very frequently, parents second-guess why their baby is crying during sleep training. They feel guilty and, looking for an out, they imagine that their baby is sick or teething or hungry. It is important to rule out legitimate health reasons for a baby's crying such as otitis (ear infection) or upper respiratory infection (head and chest colds), but it would be impossible to address all the many fears and doubts parents may have. A few common questions include:

"What if he's hungry?"

The specter of a miserably hungry baby crying out in the night hangs over most parents on the eve of their sleep work. Parents are somehow not reassured upon hearing again that a three-to-four-month-old baby who weighs at least twelve pounds can get through an eleven-to-twelve-hour period of nighttime sleep without a feeding. They have become so accustomed to feeding their baby at regular intervals through the night that this seems incredible to them.

Babies are creatures of habit. And they are smart. On the first night without his middle-of-the-night feeding your baby probably *is* a little hungry and is expecting to be fed. He cries because he knows he will be fed. But he doesn't need to eat. Giving up the middle-of-the-night feeding is not easy for your baby; it is stretching him. But almost immediately he will naturally begin to eat more during the day and he will not be hungry at night.

If your baby is like Leslie's, needing only one minute or less of nursing before falling back to sleep, it is easy to see that he is not actually hungry. But if your baby has been taking eight ounces of formula or nursing for ten to fifteen minutes several times a night, he has without doubt grown accustomed to refilling his belly throughout the night. In this case, we do not recommend doing sleep work all in one fell swoop, particularly if your baby is only three to four months old. Rather, you can first help your baby to learn the skill of falling asleep on his own at bedtime. Then you can gradually cut down on his night feedings. Given the option, some parents choose to wake their babies for one night feeding before they go to bed themselves. Having slept from 7:30 or 8:00 P.M., babies typically are so soundly asleep at eleven or twelve at night that they wake up only partially, then fall directly back to sleep after a feeding. Even though he is still getting this one night feeding, the fact that you are waking him up instead of the other way around makes your message consistent. Once your other goals are accomplished, you can eliminate this late-night snack.

Some parents prefer to train their babies gradually to expect less during their nighttime feedings, although this method usually takes longer. They continue to feed their babies when they cry at night, but diminish the number of ounces, or minutes on each breast, until a feeding is so minimal that it is clear their baby no longer needs it.

"What if he is teething?"

Parents regularly invoke teething to avoid sleep training. The truth is, babies are teething throughout this entire period. Unless your baby's tooth is actually just cutting the gum, or his gums are inflamed, there is no need to interrupt or forestall sleep work. If the erupting tooth is obviously giving your baby pain, consult your pediatrician about options for relieving your baby's discomfort.

"What if he is cold?"

A baby's room at night should be kept dark and comfortably cool. Not warm. Windows can be left open during naptime and nighttime. Typically, parents overdress their babies and keep them altogether too warm. Babies at this age can live at the same temperature as their parents do. And fresh night air can actually help babies to breathe more easily.

"What if he needs a new diaper?"

Changing a baby's diaper almost inevitably will bring him wide-awake. But if your baby has a bowel movement, it is important to change his diaper. If your baby's diaper is wet, it is not necessary to change it unless it is soaking or leaking. If you are using cloth diapers, it can be a good idea to double-diaper your baby at night or consider using an absorbent disposable diaper just during these nights of sleep training. In any case, keep the room dark during a diaper change and try to keep socializing to a minimum.

"What if he throws up from crying so much?"

Vomiting during sleep training is not the norm but it does happen. As long as your baby is not sick or feverish, you can proceed in all good conscience. It may help to keep in mind that babies do not have the same emotional response to vomiting as do older children. It makes him uncomfortable, it is not pleasant, but it is not upsetting to him. If your baby does throw up, go to him right away. Bring a warm face cloth with you. Keep the room in semi-darkness. You or your spouse can wash your baby while the other changes his crib sheets. Take a little extra time to settle your baby down again, but don't feed him. If you react with great distress and fuss, your baby may learn that this is a surefire way to get your attention. Say good-night, leave the room, and proceed with your plan.

"What if he loses his pacifier?"

The pacifier can be more hindrance than help during sleep work. You can try to increase your baby's chances of finding his pacifier on his own by putting three or four of them in his crib. Or, you can retrieve his pacifier for him during a check-in. But don't find it for him more than three times, otherwise this may develop into a fixed pattern. Another route to consider is weaning him of the pacifier for sleep purposes, which will further encourage him to find his own self-soothing techniques. Many babies who use a pacifier during the early months naturally turn to sucking their fingers or thumb. This is a fine and ever-available way for a baby to soothe himself to sleep.

"What if he rolls over onto his back and gets stuck like a turtle?"

The same advice goes for this as for the pacifier. You can turn your baby over during check-ins but only do this three times. After that you have to let him learn to settle himself to sleep on his back or roll over by himself. During the day you can help your baby to practice flipping himself over from his back to his stomach so that eventually he will be able to find his most comfortable position for sleep on his own.

"What if my baby is whimpering but not really crying? Does that count when I am timing?"

A baby's heart-tugging but not heart-wrenching whimpers should be heard as the background noises to his sleep work, the sounds he makes as he learns a new way to settle himself to sleep. Do not count whimpering as true crying when you are timing your waiting interval.

"What if my baby seems upset the following day?"

Although many parents fear that they will see recrimination in their baby's eyes in the morning after a night of sleep work, these fears are more projection than not. However, we are not saying that this isn't hard for your baby. It is. He is working hard at learning a new skill. It is stretching him. And it can be uncomfortable and even upsetting to him. Some babies will seem out of sorts during the days following sleep training. Often they are in fact more tired, or somewhat disoriented by the change in their routine. Indulge your baby during the day. Hold him more. Make him as comfortable as you can. We have never seen this kind of upset behavior as other than a temporary response, and it will not negatively affect the bond you have with your baby.

"What if my baby is sick? Can sleep training make him sick?"

Neither sleep training nor crying can make a baby sick. They cannot bring on a fever, cold, or ear infection. Sometimes, however, a couple will start sleep work only to realize sometime in the course of it that their baby is sick. This can induce intense guilt in parents and some couples will make an incorrect connection between crying and illness. If your baby becomes sick during sleep training, this is purely an unfortunate coincidence. In this case, stop all sleep work and tend to your sick baby as much as he needs. Once cleared medically, you can resume sleep training.

"What if I've been true to form for two weeks and still there is no change or progress?"

If sleep training is taking longer than two weeks, if you are seeing no improvement or only consistently erratic patterns in your baby's sleep, it's important to check with your pediatrician. Sometimes a baby will develop a subtle medical problem that manifests itself with sleep problems. Sometimes a baby will develop an intolerance for the formula he is taking, sometimes he will develop allergies, sometimes he will suffer from mild ear infections which worsen when he is lying down. In any case, it's important to get the okay from the pediatrician before you continue with sleep training.

"What if I blow it one night, give in, and nurse him to sleep. Have I ruined it?"

This does confuse your child and it may prolong the process but most parents falter at one point or another during the course of sleep work. Be gentle on yourself. Pick up the pieces and get ready again. Your baby is still able to learn. Remind yourself of your goals, for both you and your baby. Success depends on consistency but it also depends on how wholeheartedly you proceed.

∾ EARLY MORNING WAKINGS

"Keith is doing amazingly well now," Alicia proudly reports two weeks after our sleep session. "It was hard but we did it. Three bad nights of crying and now he's sleeping through the night! I put him to bed an hour after I get home at night so usually that's about eight or eight-thirty. The only thing is, he wakes up like clockwork at five-thirty in the morning. At that point I feel like I have to go to him. I think he must be starving because he guzzles his bottle down in minutes. And then he's so bright and wide-eyed that it's hard to think about putting him back to bed."

Early morning wakings are one of the most difficult parts of sleep training. Your baby has slept through five-sixths of his night. He is able to awaken now to an alert state. Any waking before 6:00 A.M. can be treated as a night waking. Your baby has not had his full cycle of sleep. Nine or ten hours may seem like enough, but it is not. Deprived of one to two hours of sleep each night, he will soon become chronically overtired and this will negatively affect his overall sleep habits. "Sleep begets sleep" is also true in the reverse. Insufficient sleep begets a disrupted sleep schedule.

Many parents opt to deal with this early morning waking problem only *after* they have gotten a few of their other sleep training goals accomplished. This can be fine short-term while you are working on some other aspect of his sleep. But losing that last hour and a half or two hours of his nighttime sleep tends to disrupt his entire schedule of sleep. So remember, within the guidelines we have established, you get what you shoot for. If you accept 5:00 or 5:30 A.M. as morning, so will your baby. Try not to let guilt undermine your goals. You are not doing your baby a favor by picking him up or nursing him at five in the morning.

ᴄᴏ NAPS AND SCHEDULES

"Justin's nighttime sleep isn't really the problem," says Jane. "He's seventeen weeks old and it's hard to get him to sleep at night but once he's down, he's down. Sometimes he wakes up once but I can deal with that. It's the daytimes that are killing me. He never really naps. He takes twenty-minute catnaps but then he's up and ready to go again. I think he must be exhausted, but he fights sleep."

Many of the same guidelines apply to daytime as to nighttime sleep work. It is important to treat a nap much the same as you treat bedtime in the evening. During sleep training especially, we discourage letting your baby catch naps on the go, in the swing, car seat, or stroller. Instead, always try to put your baby in his crib for his nap. You can use an edited version of your nightly bedtime routine in the day: clean diapers, a story or song, a bottle or nursing. Keep your baby's room dark, comfortably cool, and quiet. While your baby may have been able to sleep during a party or in his playpen during the first few months of life, this no longer holds true. Your baby can and will be awakened from a nap. So make the conditions conducive to uninterrupted sleep.

By three to four months some babies take two naps of two hours each; others, three to four forty-five-minute naps. The morning nap usually begins one and a half to two and a half hours after the morning waking and can last from one to two hours. Trust that your baby is ready for sleep and do not wait for signs that he is tired. While frequent short naps are fine as long as he is getting a full night of sleep, longer naps provide him with more hours of deep sleep. The afternoon nap can start three to four hours after he awakens from his first nap. This usually lasts one or two hours as well.

When parents report that their babies won't take naps, we ask them to tell us their baby's entire schedule of sleeping. It's helpful to look at the big picture to see how the pieces fit together. Usually a baby who is not napping well during the day, is also not getting enough sleep at night. A baby's daytime and nighttime sleep are interrelated. One affects the other. Once a baby has begun to sleep well during the night, he will often slide into a regular schedule of naps during the day with only minimal help from you. If this is not the case for your baby, you may need to follow a similar sleep training plan to help him sleep well during his daytime naps.

Your approach to daytime naps depends in part on how bad your baby's sleep situation is, but it also depends on how you are feeling. Doing the whole package of sleep work at once is the easiest way for some parents to proceed. The benefits of doing the exact same thing whenever you put your baby to bed—early morning, daytime, bedtime, or middle of the night—is that he gets a consistent and clear message and many opportunities to learn the same lesson in the course of a twenty-four-hour period. Other parents find the prospect of listening to their baby cry both night and day untenable. These couples know themselves well enough to recognize the limits to their tolerance and choose to work on daytime sleep only after nighttime sleep has been regulated. Either of these two plans can work.

When you decide to take on naptime sleep work, there are two things that are a little different from the plan we outlined for nighttime: Check-ins should be especially brief. Naptime should be limited to one hour when it is interrupted by long spells of crying.

Checking in is typically more disruptive to a baby during his nap than it is at night. You may even want to consider not checking in at all during naptime. Some mothers check in verbally from outside the door, saying "Shhhh. Time to go to sleep. Mommy's here. Go to sleep."

Sometimes babies will cry for ten or fifteen minutes, then sleep for an hour or two. Other times they will fall asleep without a fuss only to awaken after twenty minutes. Obviously, this is not a complete nap. If your baby cries for ten minutes and then sleeps for twenty and then cries for the remaining thirty minutes until the full hour is met and you get him up, you may feel as if you are giving him mixed messages. But even though the lesson your baby needs to learn is not contained in an individual crying episode, the message ultimately gets through.

One Family's Story

Elizabeth and Jonathan's baby, Lucy, has been growing and developing beautifully. At fourteen weeks, she weighed fifteen pounds, took both breast milk and formula, and had recently learned to roll over. She was laughing and vocalizing and was a very sociable baby. It had been two weeks since Lucy had started going to day care three times a week, up from twice, and she had adjusted well to that.

Elizabeth's bedtime routine with Lucy included listening to a lullaby tape, reading a story, and nursing her to sleep. Bedtime was eight o'clock at night and Lucy was sleeping until six-thirty in the morning with only one night waking. Then for a week straight she woke up two or three times every night and it began to take longer and longer to get her back to sleep. On the night before Jonathan had an important meeting at work, Lucy woke up four times.

Elizabeth had hoped this pattern would pass, but it didn't look like it was going that way. She and Jonathan realized they would have to intervene or things would only worsen. So she and her husband geared up for "the crying thing." Elizabeth and Jonathan's decision to do sleep training was a mutual one, and they were committed to making it work. Anticipating the worst, they decided to start the process on a Friday night. They decided to work on Lucy's nighttime sleep first and to allow her naps to take their own course for now. Here's how it went:

NIGHT ONE—FRIDAY

Jonathan comes home from the office early. He is tired but happy to be home with his wife and delighted to see Lucy, who always lights up when she sees her father. Elizabeth is anxious at the prospect of letting Lucy cry that night. She has prepared an early dinner but doesn't feel hungry. She starts Lucy's bedtime routine at 7:30 P.M.

At 7:45 Lucy is calm and quiet on Elizabeth's shoulder. Jonathan kisses Lucy good-night and Elizabeth takes her into her room. She reads her *Pat the Bunny*, turns off the light, then nurses her in the rocking chair. The room is mostly dark, one corner dimly illuminated by a night-light. For the first time, instead of waiting until Lucy is sound asleep at her breast, Elizabeth puts her in her crib awake, and says, "Good-night, Lucy. It's time to go to sleep now. I love you." And then Elizabeth walks out, shutting the door as she always has. It is 8:05 P.M.

Lucy screams. Elizabeth looks at Jonathan as if to say "I can't do this." She starts for Lucy's door but Jonathan holds her arm, saying, "Let's try." He checks his watch and leads Elizabeth into the living room. They sit on the couch and listen to Lucy cry. They can't pretend to distract themselves, so they watch the clock. Elizabeth and Jonathan had decided they would try to wait for ten minutes before their first check-in. As the ten-minute mark approaches, Elizabeth and Jonathan decide that Jonathan will go in to Lucy this first time.

When Jonathan goes into the room Lucy quiets momentarily but then cries even harder when she isn't picked up. Jonathan finds Lucy's pacifier and tries to give it to her, but she is crying too hard to take it. At this, Jonathan rubs her back and says "Mommy and Daddy are right outside. Go to sleep, honey." Then he leaves the room, shutting the door. Lucy is wailing.

Meanwhile, Elizabeth feels slightly panicked at the sound of Lucy crying. She can't decide which is more painful for her—to be left listening to Lucy's cries or to go to Lucy herself and not be able to pick her up.

"What was she doing?" she asks her husband.

Jonathan replies in an uncertain voice, "She's sweaty. Her eyes are puffed. She's definitely pissed off. I'm not sure if the check-in method is good for her. It seems cruel to walk out on her."

"We can't *not* check on her, Jon!" Elizabeth insists.

"Okay, okay," Jonathan agrees, "Let's keep doing it."

As Lucy's cries continue Elizabeth's becomes more anxious. She says she can't bear to hear Lucy crying anymore. Jonathan says he will go to Lucy the next time and tells Elizabeth to go for a walk.

Lucy continues to cry, but somewhat less intensely. This time, after waiting for twelve minutes, Jonathan goes in again. He whispers, "Shhh, Lu-Lu, it's okay," but his words seem lost under her cries. Lucy is turning her head back and forth, rubbing her face on the sheet. Her blanket is in a ball at the bottom of her crib. Jonathan straightens it, rubs her back, and then leaves the room with a sigh. He checks his watch and goes into the kitchen. Lucy is still crying.

Elizabeth returns from her hallway walk and tenses when she hears Lucy's cries. Jonathan calls to his wife from the kitchen. He has taken a pint of ice cream from the freezer and is chipping at it with a spoon. He puts it in the microwave to soften it and then they both eat spoonfuls while standing at the kitchen counter. All of a sudden Lucy's crying stops. Elizabeth and Jonathan look at the clock. The last interval lasted eight minutes. It has been a total of thirty-three minutes since bedtime. After Lucy has been quiet for five minutes Jonathan relaxes, but Elizabeth is still anxious. She wants to go into Lucy's room to make sure that Lucy is alright. Jonathan doesn't think this is a good idea and asks her not to, but Elizabeth says she will not be able to relax unless she does. Jonathan knows Elizabeth well enough to know this is true and agrees. Elizabeth stealthily turns the door handle to Lucy's room and tiptoes in. Lucy is asleep at the end of her crib, holding on to her blanket, her bottom high in the air. Her breathing is sure and steady and the sight of her calms Elizabeth immediately. When Elizabeth comes out into the light of the living room she and Jonathan embrace.

On this first night Lucy fell asleep during her third interval of crying. She experienced a lot of new things during the thirty-three minutes of being awake and on her own; among them probably frustration, anger, the sense of being separate from her mother and father, the physicality of very hard crying, the feeling of moving around in her crib, finding her blanket, rubbing her face on the sheet, finding a comfortable position, and finally settling down. One way or the other she found some way of soothing herself. Perhaps it was the rubbing motion of her face on the crib sheet or sucking on her blanket. Some babies suck their thumbs or twirl their hair, some nuzzle a blanket or a stuffed animal, some grunt and chant. Some babies cry to block out the world, to let out their tension and then quickly become ready for sleep. The critical point is that each baby needs to find his own way.

Elizabeth and Jonathan, though anxious and somewhat ambivalent about this undertaking, worked together well. Later that night they will be tested further. Sticking to a difficult plan can challenge even the most compatible of couples. After polishing off the ice cream, Elizabeth and Jonathan watch television for an hour and then decide to go to bed. It is 10:00 P.M.

At 2:05 A.M. Lucy wakes with a scream. Elizabeth wakes instantly. Jonathan snores. Elizabeth considers waking him but holds back. For the moment she decides not to wake him because she knows he has been under a lot of extra stress lately and needs his sleep more than she does. She gets up, taking her watch with her, and goes to the bathroom. After four minutes of listening to Lucy's escalating cries, Elizabeth's jaw is clenched. Six minutes to go. Elizabeth tweezes her eyebrows, trying to distract herself with the pain of each pluck. Then, she edges toward Lucy's room and stands at her door. At ten minutes Elizabeth is relieved to be able to go to her baby. Lucy is now on the other end of her crib, crying, facedown. Her sheet is wet with tears. Elizabeth moves her toward the center of her crib, where it is dry.

Lucy is hot and sweaty but quiets at the sight of her mother. Elizabeth feels tears welling up inside of her. She pats Lucy gently in the semidarkness. Elizabeth feels conflicted but encouraged by Lucy's calm and forces herself to stick to the plan, saying "It's night-night time, Lu-Lu. I love Lu. Go to sleep." Then she walks out of the room, checking her watch. It's two-seventeen. Lucy begins to howl.

On the verge of crying herself, Elizabeth goes into her

bedroom and shakes Jonathan. Jarred from sleep, he is disoriented.

"How can you sleep through this?" Elizabeth hisses. "You wouldn't wake up even if Lucy were choking to death! Why do I have to be the responsible one?"

"What time is it?" Jonathan asks, still waking up. "Do you want me to go in to her? How long has she been crying? Why didn't you wake me?"

"No, I don't want you to go to her!" Elizabeth retorts. "I want you to tell me *how* you can sleep through this!"

"Shit, Liz, I'm sorry! I guess I'm tired," says Jonathan. "You could have woken me up."

Elizabeth's hard-edged demeanor suddenly shatters and she is crying. Jonathan holds her and strokes her hair.

"Now both my girls are crying," Jonathan says. "Shall I check the time when you started?"

Elizabeth laughs through her tears. She and Jonathan talk quietly, holding each other as they listen to Lucy cry and watching the digital clock as it glows and flickers in the dark. Lucy's cries fill the apartment. Just before the second waiting interval of twelve minutes Lucy stops crying. Elizabeth and Jonathan can't believe it. They settle into a comfortable position in bed and begin to relax. Then Lucy cries again. Elizabeth tenses and Jonathan groans. Jonathan says he'll go in but Elizabeth remembers that they need to begin the timing all over again after an episode of quiet if the crying time was shorter than the full interval. They start from time zero. Lucy cries for another six minutes and then stops. It's 2:34 A.M. Elizabeth and Jonathan try to go back to sleep themselves, but they are both restless. They toss and turn. Jonathan falls asleep within half an hour but it is closer to 4:00 A.M. before Elizabeth lapses into sleep.

Lucy cries out. Elizabeth wakes and looks at the clock. It is 5:05 A.M. This time Elizabeth doesn't hesitate to wake Jonathan. They stay in bed and listen to Lucy cry, watching the clock. In seven minutes Lucy stops crying and without even trying to, everyone falls immediately to sleep until 7:20 A.M. when Lucy calls out again. Elizabeth is out of bed in a flash. She picks Lucy up and holds her close, saying, "Good morning, sweetness!" They have survived the first night.

NIGHT TWO—SATURDAY

The second night progresses in much the same way except that Lucy is beginning to be very overtired as are both Elizabeth and Jonathan. Lucy's cries are just as difficult to listen to, but they do not last quite as long. After the third waking of the night, Elizabeth feels a strong desire to trash the whole process, to apologize to Lucy, to save her, nurse her, rock her to sleep. But Jonathan reminds Elizabeth of their friends' baby, who is still waking two and three times a night. He is almost two years old.

NIGHT THREE—SUNDAY

On the third night Lucy's total crying time at her bedtime drops to eight minutes. She wakes only once in the middle of the night and goes back to sleep after five minutes of crying.

NIGHT FOUR—MONDAY

Elizabeth and Jonathan are hopeful. Lucy settles herself down to sleep after crying for eight minutes. But one hour after bedtime she wakes up and cries more loudly than she ever has. This goes on for close to an hour with four check-ins, throwing Elizabeth and Jonathan into a tailspin. Lucy has never done this before. "Is she sick? Has she snapped? Are we being bad parents?" they ask themselves.

It is frequently at this point that parents decide they will not continue with sleep training. They are overtired, overwrought, and overwhelmed. They feel their efforts are not panning out and begin to doubt the process altogether. Their workweek demands hang over them and, desperate for sleep themselves, they want to cut their losses and get some sleep no matter what. They go to their baby and feel they are at last able to do what their instincts have been telling them to do all along—to hold and rock and soothe their crying infant. Often they are angry at us for putting them through this ordeal. They put off sleep training for a few days or weeks or, perhaps, indefinitely.

On night four, during Lucy's hour-long cry, Elizabeth and Jonathan take turns going in to Lucy every ten minutes. Finally she quiets and then sleeps from 9:20 P.M. through the night until 6:50 A.M. Elizabeth wakes up twice during the night, anticipating Lucy's cries. Once, at 3:15 A.M., she creeps into Lucy's room to check on her and finds that all is well. What began as a setback proves to be Lucy's longest sleep through the night.

NIGHTS FIVE, SIX, AND SEVEN—TUESDAY . . .

Nights five and six unfold much as night four, but with significantly shorter crying spells. By the seventh night Lucy cries only three minutes at bedtime and then sleeps through the night from 8:05 P.M. until 7:35 A.M. It seems a miracle.

In one week Elizabeth and Jonathan helped Lucy go from a patchy nine hours of sleep with two and three night wakings to a full eleven and a half hours of straight sleep with minimal crying at bedtime. During the process of sleep training Elizabeth has become aware that Lucy's cries touch on wounds from her own past and provoke significant anxiety for her. When Jonathan is able to sleep through Lucy's cries it can make Elizabeth particularly upset. This too is linked to her past. When Jonathan is awake and participating in the process, however, his comparative calm and confidence in the process of sleep training is helpful to Elizabeth. Most importantly, Elizabeth has learned that if she can tolerate Lucy's crying for short periods without going to her, then Lucy is able to fall asleep on her own. Very soon Lucy will not cry at all and she will even be pleased to be put to bed.

Taking care of children requires unending patience, energy, and creativity. It can be joyful and fulfilling but it is always demanding. Add helping to care for your home and spouse, a job or part-time work, friends and other family members to the equation, and getting through a single day becomes a challenge. If you are trying to juggle all this on nights of broken sleep, you are most probably at wits' end. Parenting all day is hard enough. Parenting night and day is asking too much of yourself.

If your five-month-old baby is still waking up throughout the night and splintering your sleep, it's no wonder you have become depleted, impatient, tense. Babies who don't get enough sleep are more needy, more easily frustrated, and generally harder to care for during the day. When they are overtired for long periods of time their development may be compromised. The long-range effects of letting a child go without learning how to get to sleep and stay asleep are far worse than the nights of crying entailed in sleep training.

As we help mothers and couples get through the often heart-wrenching process of sleep training we try to adapt the plan to fit the family. Often we will tinker with the plan as we go along, troubleshooting with the parents for their areas of conflict or resistance. The mothers are encouraged to call us between weekly sessions if they need to. Many times parents simply need to hear encouragement and to have someone else reassure them that progress is occurring.

Helping parents to help their babies sleep well goes most smoothly when we can talk them through it face-to-face and devise a tailor-made plan. We have tried here to put in writing the essential framework to sleep training, the myriad questions that come up, and the kind of hand-holding encouragement that most parents need. But a book cannot communicate entirely this personal approach. Although many couples manage on their own, the support and objective perspective of a third person helps in troubleshooting. Ideally this would be someone who has been through a similar process.

A lot of the mothers in our groups become defensive and angry when we suggest change to them—even more so when we recommend letting their babies cry. But once these same mothers' babies are sleeping through the night they feel both relief and gratitude for the guidance and support. Over the years the parents with whom we've worked have given us glowing reports of the positive effects of sleep training. Their children are able to go to bed happily and easily and sleep soundly through the night.

*   *   *

Babies thrive on regular schedules and on plenty of sleep. They feel better when their parents are in control. Structure gives babies a sense of safety and predictability. Comfortable in an established routine and able to fall asleep on his own, a baby no longer needs to battle before bed. The bedtime routine becomes a precious and soothing time together at the end of each day.

Parents who help their babies learn to sleep through the night report having more confidence, energy, and patience themselves. Many say that their children's moods are significantly improved. Once a baby's sleep is regulated, his days are spent playing, learning, and loving more happily. A good night's sleep for your child is a gift to the whole family.

SEVEN

The Legacy of Your Own Mother
Old Conflicts, New Connections

By the time your baby says "Mama, Mama," naming and claiming you forever, you will already have begun to inextricably weave "Mother" into the fabric of your identity. Integrally woven into that same cloth is your own mother, as she is now and as she was when you were a child. As you begin to think about yourself as a mother, it becomes especially important to look at the model your mother was for you and at the early relationship you had with her. This process can help you to recognize the vital ways your mother has supported and nurtured you and the strengths in her you wish to emulate. But it can also be painful, as you think about the ways she let you down or hurt you. For some, it may trip fears and anxieties about her eventual loss, or renew grief over her untimely death.

The process of understanding the defining influence your mother has had on you will continue throughout your life, but it may flare with emotion as you first step

189

into a domain that was hers. No matter how you are feeling about your mother, we urge you to begin to reflect on the place she holds in your heart. This may seem purely an exercise in looking back, but the goal of your exploration is also about the future. It will affect how you mother your baby, how you feel about yourself as a mother, and how you construct your family life. It is meant to help you become the kind of mother you would most like to be.

The temperature has dropped. Daylight ends at four o'clock in the afternoon these days. The anticipation of winter holidays and festivities, family gatherings and traditions is heightened this year for the women in our group by the presence of their new babies. The mothers peel off their layers and make themselves and their babies comfortable. The windows, like mirrors, reflect the group, and there is a cozy, protected sense to being inside together.

"I'm almost afraid to say this," Jessica begins, "but Nell and I have had a wonderful week. I think she may finally be past her colicky stage!"

Everybody claps. Jane, who is sitting next to Jessica, leans over and tickles Nell, saying, "We are so glad you're a happy girl now!" Nell gives her a big, toothless smile in return.

The storm of Nell's newborn stage has passed and Jessica has begun to relax, to feel more confident and playful and to rejoice in her role as mother. Three months old now, her unpredictable, often inconsolable, infant has changed into a smiling, cuddly baby. Nell still needs Jessica in the most primal way—to be held and fed and rocked and soothed—but her crying has tapered off dramatically and she can more easily respond to every bit of nurturing.

Jessica continues. "It's like night and day. She is the sweetest thing on earth now. I'm so relieved. I finally feel like a good mother. In fact, sometimes I feel almost perfect."

Life with a settled baby can be profoundly soothing, a harmonious circle of nurturing and affection between mother and child. Many women in our groups say they feel like perfect mothers when their babies are four to five months old. It is at this period that a first-time mother may think she will be able to perfectly provide for and protect her little one, sparing her or him from the pains and hurts of her own childhood, repeating only the best parts, and doing everything right.

"I remember adoring my mother," Jessica responds. "She was beautiful. She still is. But I always wanted more of her. My sisters and I have a running joke about her: 'Mom never worked outside the home—so where *was* she?' That's an exaggeration, of course. I mean, she was there. But she was a whirlwind. She never stopped. I know she must have been juggling like mad. I was the second of three girls. We were born right in a row—bang, bang, bang. One a year. I don't know how she did it. It's hard work. I mean, I can barely handle one baby. The thing is, my mother did the *job* well. She cooked balanced meals. That was a big thing for her, that we were properly fed. And she kept the house clean. But I remember feeling lonely for her. I don't want Nell to feel that way."

At this, Leslie remarks, "I grew up in a household that sounds like the opposite of yours. There were three children too, but supper was usually something out of a can and our house was a mess. My mother says she didn't care about appearances but I think she was overwhelmed. Dad was gone a lot for work and Mom needed help. So I became her self-appointed 'Little Cleaner.' Keeping order became very important to me.

"To this day, I'm still that way," Leslie continues. "I get anxious when the apartment is a mess. There are times when I find myself ignoring Eric to clean up. That upsets me but the weird thing is, I can't stop myself. Sometimes when I think about it, I blame my mother. But I know it's not that simple. I'm beginning to see that you can't win as a mother."

Part of growing up is understanding that parents are *not* perfect. By the time you are a mother yourself you probably have accepted this fact of life. But for a new mother, the past becomes amplified. In the quiet and dark of a 2:00 A.M. feeding, half-awake and half-asleep, a new mother can be transported to a sense of herself when she was a child, even to a time before words. In her more wakeful hours, without fully realizing why, the new mother may see her own mother through childlike eyes, wanting again to be perfectly loved.

Over the course of the first year of new motherhood, there may be a natural unfolding of your new identity. But you may also begin to feel stuck in patterns that you don't like. Or you may feel somewhat alienated from yourself or from your baby or from your husband without knowing why. This is when the journey back to your own mother is vitally important. There is no single recipe for motherhood but there is a lot to be said for a healthy dose of self-awareness.

When she was a child Jessica didn't get as much loving attention as she wanted from her mother. From a very young age Leslie felt the need for more order in her home.

Now as mothers themselves, Jessica and Leslie can identify more with their own mothers—they each have experienced the challenges of motherhood. This personal experience has softened their criticisms of their own mothers. But it has also made them particularly sensitive to their own childhood hurts.

Most adults try to ignore and even to deny their childlike emotions. But as a new mother, it can be helpful to explore and understand these very significant feelings. At this point, we ask each group member to think about what makes a perfect mother, based on what she had, or wished she had had. According to this group the perfect mother:

- is nurturing, caring, and loving during each stage of her child's development

- is involved in a loving, supportive relationship with her partner

- does not try to control her child or make her the sole focus of her life

- maintains active interests outside the home, but never at the expense of her child's needs

- does not try to fulfill her own unresolved needs through her child

- encourages independence in her child but can accept inevitable regressions

- consistently knows her child, listens, is fair and respectful

- gives her child the freedom to unfold as he or she naturally will; accepts and loves her child for who she or he is and applauds her child's unique abilities and gifts

- knows how to set fair and appropriate limits
- has never had a problem with drugs, alcohol, or depression; is never abusive
- provides unconditional love

Quickly the point is made. It may be childlike to expect parents to be perfect, but it is human nature to yearn to be perfectly loved. Every woman carries with her an image of the perfect mother. But there is no such thing. No one is infallible. Including your mother. Including you.

∾ BLUEPRINTS AND ROLE MODELS

"I don't know what my mother was like when I was a baby. No one really does, do they?" Ronnie asks. "But sometimes I'll hear myself talk or sing to Elyse and the sound of my voice and my choice of words will be just like my mother's, from a long time ago. And then I get such a sense of her influence on me and realize that I am that person for Elyse now. I so much want to be a good mother for her too."

There are an infinite number of ways to be a good mother. Above all, a good mother is loving and tries her best. Caring for a baby is a uniquely creative and passionate act. But it is also an imperfect art in an imperfect world.

"My mother and I are a lot alike," says Alicia. "I realize

that more and more. I didn't *try* to be like her. It's genes, I think."

Many women attribute their most fundamental character traits to their mothers—their sense of humor, their self-esteem, their sense of morality, their ability to give and receive love, to listen and communicate, their desire to strive for goals. When these women become mothers themselves, the comparisons become even more powerful.

Some women think they are destined to become blueprints of their own mothers, repeating patterns automatically; others feel compelled to reject their mothers' choices outright; others hope to live up to their mothers' examples. Whether she is alive or not, a close confidante or a thorn in her daughter's side, down the block or across the country, a woman's mother is the template from which she creates herself as a mother. From a very early age, a young girl identifies closely with her mother and copies her behavior and her mannerisms.

"My mother was always there for me," says Jane. "I know she has her own feelings of inadequacy but she has always been loving and supportive of me. I admire how she has done things. I think she is the main reason I didn't go back to work. My husband couldn't believe I wanted to stay home. It surprised me too because I've always loved my work. But I wanted to be that same kind of old-fashioned mother for Justin that my mother was for me."

"That makes me want to cry," says Alicia. "The theme of my childhood was that Mom didn't have time for us. She went back to school when I was one. Then she worked constantly. When she became successful, she traveled a lot for her work. She still does. She was at some convention when Keith was born. Typical."

Alicia pauses and then continues. "But, I have to say

that I admire my mother too. She is one of the most intelligent, elegant women I know. She has a great deal of presence and strength. She taught us—and showed us—that we could do anything we put our minds to. My sister is a doctor. My brother is a professor. I'm a lawyer. But I always wanted to establish myself before having kids so I wouldn't be caught low on the career ladder as a new mother."

"Instead of living it herself, I think my mother expected to live through her children," says Marta. "I know that was pretty typical for her generation. Mothers were praised for being self-sacrificing then. She thought it was being totally giving, but actually it was something of a burden. Mom and Dad were both critical. They had very high expectations for us. One of the things I want to be sure to give Sarah is my unconditional love."

Like her mother, Jane wants to be consistently available to her son. Like her mother, Alicia has chosen to juggle career and motherhood but aspires to balance better than her mother did. Marta, reacting against her mother's style, wants to give her daughter unconditional, uncritical love. All three women are using their perceptions of their own mothers as guides in how, or how not, to raise their children and structure their lives.

Many of the choices you make will also reflect the changes in the times since your mother's young adulthood, including today's changed economic pressures and opportunities for women in the workplace, the influence that feminism has had on our culture, changing theories on child development and health, and the greater awareness of the psychological process of growing up. Mothering style, however, transcends generational differences. It is as unique as you are.

Key to *your* mothering style are your feelings about dependence and independence, permissiveness and control, safety and danger, giving and withholding, intimacy and the expression of feelings. Each of these has its root in your own mother's personality, her response to parenting and in her relationship with you. Much of the way you have developed as a woman comes from having watched her. As a child, you studied her intently and learned from her happiness and her sadness, from her sense of satisfaction and regret, from her relationships with her husband and children, from her place in the home and out in the world.

∽ VOICES FROM THE PAST

Many mothers say they remind themselves of their own mothers in the ways they hold, rock, soothe, and talk to their babies. Caring for your baby can recall the tactile, sensory experience of your own babyhood. Images, sounds, even the smell of baby powder, can unleash previously unavailable memories, pictures, flashes of feelings, both sweet and painful.

New motherhood is a time of life when many women report feeling an intense personal need for the nurturing power of their own mother. Often these expectations are a source of disappointment. If your mother comes to visit you after your baby is born, for instance, you may hope that she will mother *you* as well as help with your newborn.

"Sometimes I think I have that fantasy mother," says Jane. "My mother comes over a couple of times a week. She watches Justin, sometimes she'll straighten up, sometimes she'll cook or go to the market. She's great company. I'm a little embarrassed to admit this, but I don't think I could do it without her."

The women in the group are almost groaning with envy. Ronnie speaks for everyone when she asks, "How come your mother can give so much of herself? I mean, my mother helps me once in a while, but she's busy with her own life too."

"My mother has always given of herself. Maybe too much," Jane answers. "But my mother is alone now. My father died two years ago. I've spent a lot more time with Mom since then. And we live so close to each other it makes it easy. You know, I think my mother needs me as much as I need her. And Justin is so good for her spirits."

"You're lucky, Jane," says Jessica. "My mother and I have always been close, too. Like friends. But now, just when I could use a little extra help, she is spending less and less time with me. And Nell has been so hard. There have been times when Nell was crying and I was crying and all I wanted in the world was my mother."

"I know. I know," says Elizabeth. "And then I tell myself, 'Grow up, Liz. You are the mother now.' "

"What do you mean?" Maggie asks Elizabeth. "Is your mother not around?"

"Yes. No. I mean, she lives in D.C.," says Elizabeth. "She and my dad both just retired. They've moved into a condo and we were there visiting this weekend. I had been looking forward to it but now I wish we hadn't gone. I mean, I was stupid to expect anything different. We're supposed to go there for Christmas but now I'm totally rethinking our plans."

"What happened?" Maggie asks.

"Oh, I don't know. Nothing dramatic," Elizabeth answers. "The same old stuff, really. First it's her smoking. It's hard to ask her not to smoke in her own house. But Lucy is my priority, so I did. Her response was 'I smoked when all of you were babies. And I'm not going to stop now.' I was horrified. It seemed so mean to Lucy. So from the moment we arrived I was on the defensive.

"Then at six o'clock Dad started making drinks. Lucy was fussy and crying and I wanted to get her bath going and to start getting her ready for bed. I was kind of harried and Dad said, 'Are you sure you don't want a beer?' I could have used some help. Not a beer. I went to give Lucy a bath. I was glad to have an excuse to disappear. Jonathan was trying to be social. He had a drink with them and they were all talking. I could hear their conversation and I wondered if I had overreacted or if I was getting my period or something. After a while Mom came to find me. She was trying to be sweet but her voice was a little slurred and she smelled of cigarettes; all I wanted to do was get back in the car and go home.

"Nighttime with my parents has always been hard. They don't drink during the day. But the evening cocktail hour has been an institution in my family for as long as I can remember. It's not really an hour, though—sometimes they'll drink until they go to bed. I remember a few times Dad passed out sitting up. And there were nights when my mother had to go to bed before dinner. It was never ugly. They just kind of faded out."

"What did you do then?" Nan asks leaning closer to Elizabeth. "Who took care of you?"

"At the time I didn't think *I* needed to be taken care of. But my younger brother and sister did. I was about ten when this was happening. I'm the oldest, so I was used to helping out with them. At bedtime I read to them and tucked them in and listened for them during the night. I was their little mother. It felt pretty normal to me.

"In fact, during the day it *was* normal. It was as if nothing had happened the night before, as if nothing was wrong. Mom was herself again. And in many ways she was a great mother. She adored us. She could be loving and fun. I was devoted to her. But I came to be afraid of nighttime. It was all such a mixture of good and bad. I was always doubting my own perceptions. I think I still try to pretend their drinking is not as bad as it is. But that old feeling is still there."

We ask Elizabeth if her feelings for her mother have changed since having Lucy.

"Now that I see what it takes to be a mother, I can't believe that she drank when we were little. There was a time when I thought that it was good that I could blame alcohol for my mother's behavior. It was a great excuse: my mother wasn't there for me because she was drinking, not because she didn't love me. Then, believe it or not, I fell in love with a man who had a drinking problem. This was before Jonathan. It was a very destructive relationship and I was in it for years. He needed the help, but I was the one who ended up in therapy. And it was a good thing too—that was my salvation. My therapist was great. And the whole process of therapy was an awakening for me.

"I still love my mother. And I know my mother and father love me," says Elizabeth, her eyes filling with tears. "Oh, God, I feel like such a baby."

As Elizabeth experiences motherhood herself, she has come face-to-face with scenes from her own childhood drama and with her parents' alcoholism. Elizabeth is not alone. In every group there are parallel stories. If your mother was consumed by alcohol, work, depression, grief, or a protracted physical illness and was as a result absent or negligent in some way, you may feel similarly conflicted. In the belief that she might repair the hurt of her own unmet needs, a new mother may feel compelled to overcompensate with her baby, giving of herself even at the expense of her marriage or of her own well-being. But facing honestly and seeing clearly the mother of her past, in all her own glory and pain, is an important step toward assuming the role of mother fully. If Elizabeth can do this with the help of her partner and her baby, she may have more reasonable and flexible expectations of herself as well.

It helps Elizabeth to realize she is not alone, that other mothers are struggling as well, that their mothers were also a mixture of good and bad and that there is no such thing as the perfect mother. The process of becoming a mother has in effect helped Elizabeth to see her mother more clearly and in doing so to take important steps toward maturing and separating and dedicating herself to her new family.

"I've been sad all over again too," says Nan about her mother, who died four years before Emma's birth.

"It's hard not having my mother here for this," she continues, holding up Emma with pride. "It's like all my joy is lined with sadness. I never dealt with my mother's illness until Emma was born. And until recently I thought I was handling it all pretty well. But now it is like a floodgate bursting.

"It's hard to know how much has to do with pure grief and how much has to do with sleep deprivation," Nan continues. "Emma keeps me up a lot at night. And then when she is finally asleep I find myself upset about my mother. So I'm hardly sleeping at all and my emotions are out of control. I just wish I could talk with my mom. I miss her so much. And I wish that she could have known Emma."

Nan rocks Emma, soothing herself as she soothes her baby.

"I know just what you mean," says Jane. "Sometimes I don't know which is sadder—that my father will never know Justin, or that Justin will never know my father."

There is a great sadness when that link is lost as it takes with it part of a family's history. A lot of mothers have told us that one of their primary motivations for having a baby at a young age was to ensure a relationship between grandchild and grandparent. Having had wonderful grandparents themselves, many women wish to re-create their past in this way for their own children. And they wish to connect again with their own parents in this joyful way.

Having lost a parent through death or divorce will greatly influence your relationship with your child. The birth of your baby may bring you joy but may also bring a fresh sense of your loss. You may find yourself mourning all over again, crying over your baby's head. Your mother's death may conjure up fears of dying yourself, of leaving your baby without a mother. Her absence will most certainly increase your yearning for her companionship, help, and nurturing. Some of the women we have talked to about this have told us that, with time, their baby becomes a bridge back to their own lost mother. The very journey of motherhood, one woman told us, helped her to find her own mother again, to hear her voice again, to remember again.

⟳ YOUR MOTHER AS GRANDMOTHER

With the birth of your baby there is a great shifting of the generations. Just as your transition to motherhood is a passage into a new life phase, so is your mother's to grandmotherhood. After decades of being the mother, she must now move over, make room for you and rethink her self-concept.

She will also have to rethink her name. Your mother may choose a name to be called as a grandmother. But as likely your baby will one day invent the name that sticks. Part baby talk, part association, your mother's official appellation may become MiMi, NaNa, GeeGee, Rummy, Nonna, Nonie, Nanny, Nanna, Grummy, Mumsie, Vavoa, Puggy, Grammy, Gramma Dot, or MaMa Ginny. Eventually you may call your own mother by her grandmother name.

"My mother says she doesn't want to be called any grandmother name. She wants to be called by her first name. But I think that's too strange," says Jessica. "My older sister and I both had babies this year and I guess it's hard for Mom to accept that she's a grandmother. She's only forty-seven. We've been like sisters since I was a teenager. In fact, everyone says we still look like sisters."

Being a grandmother can be one of the most life-affirming and joyous periods in a woman's life. But in this youth-loving culture, it can as well be a difficult life phase. Your mother may already be having a hard time accepting that she is getting old. She may be in the throes of menopause. Or she may have mixed feelings about her landmark sixty-fifth birthday. She may simply not like the way "Grandma" sounds.

"My mother doesn't have the energy for a baby," says

Leslie. "She said so herself. I know she's getting old, but I don't understand why she acts afraid of the baby."

By the time she becomes a grandmother, a woman may feel no desire to undertake the nitty-gritty aspects of baby care again. She may feel liberated from those days, or she may feel out of practice, unsure of herself. Many women report their mothers saying "I don't have the patience anymore," or "This is exhausting. I've forgotten how hard it is," or "I like babies better when they're older."

A grandchild can stir up the past for the new grandmother as she relives old joys and feels again old regrets. For some women a grandchild elicits strong feelings of well-being, a sense of rebirth, new energy, and a fresh focus for their love and affections. Others experience a preoccupation with mortality, a sadness and a longing for a time when they were young mothers themselves. No matter how they present themselves, almost all carry inside of them the full range of these emotions.

As a grandmother, a woman walks something of an emotional tightrope. The new mother wants her own mother to be supportive and helpful but not intrusive or domineering; older and wiser but not dependent or needy herself; doting on and loving toward the baby but respectful of the mother's primary role and authority; happy to pass on family stories, recipes, and traditions but not overwhelming in the role of family matriarch. A grandmother is supposed to be filled with joy at the sight of her grandchild, ready to sacrifice. But, just as the perfect mother is an impossibly tall order to fill, so is that of the perfect grandmother.

"I'm the last of my siblings to have a baby," says Alicia. "Keith is Mom's fifth grandchild, so she's not exactly jumping up and down with excitement. But I'll give her this—she's much more affectionate with her grandchildren than she was with her own children. And she lavishes them with gifts."

"My mother is more focused on her own mother than on her grandaughter," says Marta. "She's sweet with Sarah but Gram takes up all of her time. She expects me to help her with Gram, but between Sarah and my work, my hands are full. It's kind of a gyp for everyone. But I think Sarah is the one who gets gypped the most."

If you are in your late twenties or thirties, your baby may have come at a time when your mother needs to help with the care of her own parents. Or, if you delayed motherhood until your late thirties or forties, your mother may be becoming dependent or needy herself. If this is the case, two powerful life passages will overlap for you—the aging and eventual loss of your parents and your early parenting years.

If your mother lives close enough to be involved on a regular basis with you and your baby, there will be more opportunities for a tangible sense of sharing as your baby grows. There will also be more chances for you to lock horns. A baby can trigger a grandmother's maternal instincts and she may be unable to take a backstage role.

"My mother keeps telling me to relax," says Ronnie. "She says I should not try to impose a schedule on my baby, that Elyse will naturally eat and sleep when she needs to. She's not big on structure or discipline. But I want to give Elyse more limits and more guidance."

"You have to be careful with limits," says Marta. "Guidance is one thing, but limits can feel very controlling. My mother made me dress just so and do my hair just so. I had to do well in school and have the right friends. It was as if who I was wasn't good enough for her. She wanted me to reflect her in the right way. And the right way was her way. The way I was accepted was through obedience. I'm afraid to be the slightest bit controlling with Sarah. I can just imagine how I might be. You know, 'Go ahead—step in the puddles! Have dessert before dinner! Mess up your room!' It'll be like my own little rebellion.

"My mother had lots of power over me," Marta goes on. "And I became Little Miss Obedience. To this day she uses money as a way to control me. She's very generous with it but expects a return. I steam at the idea of her doing that with Sarah. I'd rather she came over and get to know her, take her for a walk. I want my daughter to value real connections, not material ones. I feel very competitive with her."

"I feel that way with my stepmother sometimes," says Maggie. "She's always saying, 'I can't wait to get my hands on Jack.' And throughout my pregnancy she would say, 'How's *our* baby?' I can't begrudge her her grandchild. But I don't want to have to share Jack with her so much."

"You're lucky she says 'our,'" says Jane. "My mother says, 'How's *my* baby?'"

The group is surprised by Jane's comment and Jane holds up her hands, saying, "Yes, I know. I know. I've painted the perfect mother picture. But I guess there is some competition there, too. My mother is so in love with Justin, so attentive to every detail of his life. It's like she's *his* mother, not mine."

Sharing your baby with your mother can bring you closer, but a lot depends on how you feel about sharing with your mother to begin with. Competitive feelings are an ever-present yet rarely acknowledged dynamic in the relationship between mother and daughter. If your mother has always assumed a certain ownership of your life, you may put up defenses when it comes to sharing your baby. If she was more removed as a mother, however, you may want her involvement now more than ever.

The choices you make about your baby's care and the course of your family's life affect your mother. She may marvel at your breast feeding or try to undermine it. She may disapprove of your working or wish she had been able to do that herself. She may become closely involved with you and the grandchildren or she may not. You may be baffled by your mother's behavior at times. It may be that your perspective as a daughter obscures the complete and complicated woman your mother is. Simultaneously, your mother may be so accustomed to relating to you in a motherly way, that she is not in the habit of explaining herself to you as a woman.

To widen our circle further, this time to include the experiences and perspectives of some grandmothers, we got permission to and spoke directly with the mothers of many of the women in this group. We include here the personal stories of Jane and Alicia's mothers. In their own words each describes how it was when she was a mother of small children and how it feels to be a grandmother.

Jane's Mother

"Being a grandmother doesn't make me feel old. It makes me feel enriched. It is one of the most incredible experiences of my life. I have three granchildren. Two beautiful granddaughters and my new grandson, Justin. I cannot express the warmth and joy I feel in my heart for them.

"I didn't work outside of the home when I was raising my children. It wasn't something that most women I knew did. It wasn't something I even considered. I still feel that staying home was the right thing to do. I am only sorry that I did not pursue a career after my children were grown. Even though I have never worked outside the home, I raised my daughter to be independent and career-oriented and she is.

"My husband was away most of the time working. He wasn't even home at dinnertime. The raising of our children was completely left to me. My daughter was an amazing part of my growing up as a young mother. I was very young—twenty years old—when she was born and I had very little sense of myself. My daughter became the most important person in my life. We bonded from the beginning. And we've always needed each other intensely. In some ways she took care of me.

"Now I can see that perhaps that was a burden on Jane. It was always very hard for her to leave me to go to school. She would cry and cry. At the time I didn't have any insight into the psychology of things, but I guess I didn't want her to leave me either. It was a very powerful relationship.

"Even though she is a grown woman with her own family, I think I'll always feel like 'Jane's Mother.' It is a great part of my identity. I have a life that is separate from that role and which centers around who I am today. But I am still very much her mom, too.

"I don't want my grandchildren to become my entire life but they are undoubtedly a wonderful part of it. They love me and I love them and it's an unbelievably good feeling. Sometimes I want my grandchildren to love me more than anyone else and then I realize that the most important people in their lives are their mother and father and that is the way it should be. But it's wonderful just to know they love me very much and think I'm an important influence in their lives.

"The advice I would give to a new mother is: Have a sense of humor. Keep your expectations in perspective. Give a lot of love and support. And try to detach a little bit so that your children can grow and so you are not so intensely affected by everything that happens. And it does all happen. The best part about motherhood for me was watching my babies grow, creating and nurturing them, feeling so much love and getting love in return. Experiencing life with a child, through a child, is an amazing process."

Alicia's Mother

"I feel enthusiastic to be a grandmother. It's a rejuvenating experience. I wish my children had had children sooner. I feel warmly toward my grandchildren. They are charming and I'm glad to spend time with them when I can. But I have to admit, sometimes I get a little bored.

"I started working when I was a young mother. I liked the balance between my children and my career. I thought I juggled pretty well. We had a nanny. My husband was not interested in infants but he was a help with the diapers and the bottles. And when the children were older he read to them and was more involved.

"I always wanted to work, but I was also very fond of my children. The painful thing for me was that there was a strong social pressure against mothers who worked. This was the 1960s remember. I was regularly chewed out by my neighbors for not being part of the car pools and parents' associations.

"I wanted my daughters to learn to work. I think it is important for a woman to realize herself. I did neglect some things as a mother. But I did give my children the idea that work is rewarding and that independence is important.

"That feeling of being a mother never goes away. I still can't stand to see a movie in which children suffer. But motherhood is not my only identity. I take my work very seriously.

"It is hard when Alicia doesn't listen to me and when I realize I am not her authority regarding child care. She always has to check in with the pediatrician first if she has questions. I think not learning from their parents' experience is a peculiarly American custom. Each generation thinks their way is better. I have learned over the years that I can't do very much about the choices my children make. They have to make their own mistakes and learn from them. And I have to let go.

"The hardest part about being a grandmother for me is when a grandchild resists what I want to teach. I have one grandchild who refuses to greet people. Her mother doesn't insist on it either. I have to keep my mouth shut. That doesn't come easily.

"The advice I would give to a young mother today would be: Don't worry so much. Trust in their natural growth process. And don't worry so much when babies cry. As you become more experienced you will become more relaxed about this, too.

"The best part of motherhood for me was the companionship with my children. They were always teaching me things, bringing me home things, stretching me. I had to keep growing. It is a very creative process to raise children. All of us need to make something, to build something. It is fascinating to help to shape personalities. I also think I would have become very selfish if I didn't have children. They kept me feeling young and involved."

⌒ NEW CONNECTIONS, NEW BALANCES

The way you and your mother relate to one another has been changing and shifting from the moment you were born. There have also been dramatic changes in our society's expectations of women's roles over the last thirty years. As such, motherhood may be the first truly common experience you and your mother have shared. Most new mothers gain insight into and empathy for their mothers which they never had before. Almost all report new ways to relate with their mothers that hadn't before been possible.

"My mom was the traditional stay-at-home mother with three kids," says Leslie. "I never appreciated what that took before. Now, the idea boggles my mind. I understand why our house was upside-down most of the time and I have new sympathy and respect for my mother."

"My mother has surprised me," says Marta. "Before I got Sarah, our relationship was so antagonistic. She was jealous of me for what I have done with my life. She felt she didn't have permission to do what I am doing. With Sarah she suddenly has a respect for me that she's never had before. I don't think she expected me to be good at this."

"My mother and I talk on the phone all the time," says Ronnie. "She's been a big help to me and always helps me get perspective on things. She's been the one that makes me feel less alone in all of this, more than anyone except maybe this group. It makes me happy to share motherhood with her."

When a woman has a baby, there is often a shift in the balance of power between her and her mother. Many new mothers talk about their relationship with their mother in terms of "Before" and "After" the baby. Motherhood can be an equalizing experience, putting both women on common ground for the first time.

"I thought I would have to stand up to my mother," says Marta. "But she hasn't tried to take over with Sarah or to tell me to do things her way like I had expected. We are more like equals now."

It may be as simple as your mother coming to where you live rather than you always traveling to her. Or, that you finally learn to ask her for help. Or that she finally feels comfortable giving it. It may be a significant breakthrough in a long-standing stalemate of emotions. Or that you are communicating for the first time in years.

"I had a very old-fashioned mother and I had a lot of problems with that as an adolescent," says Leslie. "But I have to say that now that I have my own child I can understand my mother in ways that never occurred to me before. And now that I know what it takes, I'm in awe of how she got dinner on the table every night."

"I'm making a video for my father's sixty-fifth birthday from our old home movies," says Elizabeth. "I haven't looked at this stuff for years. It's amazing to see my mother as a young woman with us as little kids. She played with us and laughed and hugged us. There's one part that one of the kids must have taken cause it's from this low angle of my parents kissing and play-fighting together. I cry every time I watch that reel. It is profound for me to see my mother so happy. Especially when now I have all these other feelings about what has transpired in the meantime."

"I have felt a new sense of time passing," says Ronnie. "I was at my parents' house this weekend and we set up Elyse's crib in my childhood bedroom. At night I was singing lullabies to her and looking around my old room and I was flooded with memories. It was a very beautiful, very poignant feeling. It was about wanting to teach things to my baby that my mother taught me. About wanting to stop time. Elyse fell asleep in my arms and I just watched her sleeping for about twenty minutes. When I finally went downstairs it was very comforting to see my own mother."

Maggie wells up with tears listening to Elizabeth's and Ronnie's stories. "I know that things have been strained between me and my stepmother since Jack's birth because I want my real mother so badly. After Mom left I didn't see her for almost six years. Since then we've seen each other only for short visits. It's always been complicated between us. I can't help missing her and wanting her, but I still feel angry that she left. Now that Jack is here, Mom and I are both trying to be together more often. We don't want to waste this chance to recover a little of what we missed."

As you reach out to your mother, or she to you, you may feel that you've come full circle. Boundaries to closeness created when you were younger, which may have once been vital to your identity, may not seem quite as important anymore. The very fleeting quality to your baby's infancy may inspire a sense of urgency about making amends.

Nan encourages the women in the group to seek out their mothers, telling them, "You can't fully appreciate your mother until she's gone. And then when she is gone you realize there is no one else like her for you in the world."

If your mother is still alive, you will have the opportunity for a while to be both child and parent. Like a boat gently dipping and rising, you will rock back and forth between being a mother and being a daughter, moving from the past into the present and imagining into the future.

As a mother you experience life in a whole new way, with new eyes, through the life of your infant and child. Most adults cannot remember anything about their infancy and their first few years of life. Memories do not connect us to that primal, dependent, amorphous state. And so a first baby can become a metaphor for a lost babyhood, as powerful as poetry, transporting, evoking, and letting you imagine for the first time what it means to be an infant child and what it truly means to take care of one. New mothers look with new respect to their own mothers, with new curiosity and understanding and often with the desire to connect again.

～ THE LEGACY OF YOUR MOTHER

Our group discussion on mothers is always a serious one, full of heartfelt stories. Emotions can range from the most universally clichéd to the most profoundly meaningful. How you were mothered affects how you will be as a mother. And yet, how you will be as a mother is not set in stone. You have the potential to choose, to change, and to better understand yourself. This may require that you struggle to confront yourself and your past honestly. But motherhood offers a rare chance to readdress your childhood. The need to know your mother is also the need to know yourself. Her legacy will, in part, be handed down from you to your own child. That inheritance will be reflected in part by how your child feels about herself, the world, relationships, and, ultimately, about parenting.

EIGHT

Full Circle
Attachment and
Separation

Two weeks have passed. Chanukah and Christmas have come and gone. A new year has begun. As the women fill the room, talking together easily and casually, it is clear the group has a life of its own. This is our last session. But the women have made plans to continue meeting once a week on their own.

A baby's laugh rings out. Leslie and Eric are engaged in a game of peek-a-boo. Leslie holds a baby blanket over her face, then lowers it, saying, "Peek-a-boo!" Eric smiles with delight, his mouth opening in a wide O. Up goes the blanket again and from behind it Leslie asks "Where's Ma Ma?" Eric stares at the blanket, his expression intent and expectant. Down comes the blanket. "Peek-a-boo!" says Leslie. "Here I am!" Eric laughs a gurgling, baby, belly laugh, thrilled by the game, thrilling his mother.

Time-honored and universally loved, peek-a-boo is a game about separation and attachment. As the blanket goes up and down, like a theater curtain, Leslie disappears and then, like magic, reappears. By making a game of it, she is helping Eric learn to let go of her for a minute, showing him that if she goes away, she will always come back. Eventually Eric will even initiate peek-a-boo himself. He will hide behind his bib, a book, a curtain, only to peek out, his eyes aglow, smiling too, as if to say, "You're back! I'm back! We're together again!" In this way, he takes a turn at controlling his mother's place in his world.

Attachment and separation are the elemental issues between parent and child. Invisible, immeasurably powerful ties connect them. At times these ties will bind and pull; at times they will stretch, turn, and spin. It is a dance which lasts a lifetime.

You and your husband were probably deeply attached to your baby well before he was even born. During the course of pregnancy a mysterious, expectant relationship is formed with the life growing within. Parents-to-be often talk to their unborn baby, sing to him, "listen" to him hiccup, feel him move. Some even have a name for him. Well before their child is born, he seems to have an identity and a full, projected life of his own.

Adoptive parents also experience a prenascent attachment as they wait for the news that a baby can be theirs. They project hopes and fears on an unknown child as they prepare a nest and a place in their hearts for his homecoming. Sometimes hopes are raised only to be dashed. And yet, despite the stress of waiting and not knowing, these candidates for parenthood remain faithfully attached to the idea of a baby in their arms.

Some adoptive parents worry about the separation the child has already experienced. Some focus on the initial meeting and wonder if they will instantly love their adopted baby. But attachment is not built on first impressions and reactions. Nor does it happen at the moment of birth, that mythical bonding often described. Rather, connections between a baby and his parents are made in daily trickles and surges, as over time their relationship widens and deepens.

∽ EARLY ATTACHMENT

As you play games, smile, cuddle, and flirt with your baby, you may be filled with unparalleled feelings of love, protectiveness, awe, and pride. You may become aware of how merged with your baby you feel—psychologically, emotionally, and somehow even physically. This merged attachment, this romantic symbiosis of sorts, is exactly what your baby thrives on. He needs you to be in love with him, for you are his partner, mirror, interpreter, nurturer, savior, mother-love. It is on this base of secure dependence that a baby builds a sense of himself, and eventually, a sense of independence.

"I'm in love with Elyse, but sometimes I wonder if she really needs *me*," says Ronnie. "I mean, she seems happy in anyone's arms."

In the early weeks and months of your baby's life, although he is undoubtedly dependent on you, it may not be clear that your baby is attached specifically to you. In fact, most infants up to eight weeks appear relatively indiscriminate. They will let almost anybody hold them, change them, or give them a bottle. They look with interest at any engaging face. They do not give clear signs that they recognize their parents. It's no wonder, then, that a mother may catch herself thinking, "Would *any* competent pair of hands do?"

Although there is much that is mundane and repetitive in the care of a newborn, the job is far from custodial. Less visible than a brimming laundry basket and diaper pail at the end of the day are the myriad connections that have taken place between mother and child. During the course of one twelve-hour day, a new mother may kiss her baby more than a hundred times, look into his eyes over three hundred times, stroke and touch, cradle and pat him close to five hundred times, have dozens of "conversations" with him, and sing as many songs or nursery rhymes. This loving connection is the treasure hidden in the groundwork of a baby's daily care. It is the most important goal and the most important accomplishment of the first year. Crucial to his emotional and cognitive development, it is the foundation from which he will establish and enjoy meaningful relationships.

Most new parents would be surprised to learn how reciprocal the attachment process is and how complex and capable their infants are. There is evidence that when a newborn is a few hours old, he recognizes and gravitates toward his parents' voices and that he can use his sense of smell to differentiate his mother from other women. An infant's vision is far better than previously believed. And a baby is driven to get loving attention as surely as he is driven to be fed and to sleep.

"Sometimes I worry," says Jessica. "I mean, I bonded with Nellie right away. But during all that colic, there was a lot of unbonding going on."

A colicky infant can be grueling to cope with, upsetting and stressful to his parents. When crying and discomfort far outweigh smiling and cuddling it can be difficult to feel as though a loving relationship is developing. But colicky babies become attached just as other babies do.

And so do their parents. In fact, caring for a needy, uncomfortable, or sick infant can make a parent particularly sensitive and responsive to a baby's needs and comfort levels. As such, colic may shape part of the early relationship, but it neither limits nor defines it.

∾ AS ATTACHMENT GROWS

Your newborn's dark, round, unblinking eyes draw you in as surely as a lover's gaze. His infant yawns and stretches, his quivering hands and velvety skin invite admiration and touch. His first baby smiles, given to you and the world, ensure delight and attention. And then, sometime after his eighth week, his seduction act becomes focused on you alone. You are the one he wants. You are the one that can soothe and settle him and make him shine. No one can match you or replace you. By the time he is twelve weeks, a baby will flaunt his mother-love. When she comes into sight, he turns his head in her direction, his eyes and expression brighten, he kicks, waves his arms, makes sounds and smiles. He has come to know that this someone understands him and takes care of him. Her arms feel right, her smell is familiar and pleasurable, she knows the rhythms and pace of his days and nights.

"When Justin was tiny he would stare at me so intently and with such devotion I could do nothing but stare back," says Jane. "Now he watches me wherever I go. He tracks me like an umpire at a tennis match. His devotion is intense!"

"I know what you mean," says Alicia. "I've never felt so special in anyone's eyes."

As you and your baby begin to interact in more obvious

ways, a whole new range and layer of emotions comes into play for both of you.

✧ EARLY STRANGER ANXIETY

"Everywhere we go people fawn over Sarah and tell me she's beautiful. I get a vicarious thrill from it," says Marta.

Life with a tiny baby can give you a taste of what it might feel like to live with a movie star. Crowds of admirers press up against the nursery window to get a glimpse of the newborn beauty. Papparazzi's flashes track him. Video cameras roll around him. Everywhere you go together, your baby takes the spotlight. Even strangers stop, stare, and gush—"How adorable! How beautiful!" Your baby can command an audience in the elevator, enchant passengers on the bus, charm your friends as he moves from one adoring fan to the next. Everyone falls for him. He steals every show.

Then, quite abruptly, the baby who delighted and entertained everybody, who allowed anyone to hold him, is recoiling, clinging, and crying in alarm. Someone has admired him at too close range. Someone has tried to get him to smile. Someone has wanted to hold him.

"Emma is only thirteen weeks old," says Nan. "But she's definitely clinging to me and crying when people want to hold her. According to the books, stranger anxiety doesn't happen until much later."

The classically documented phase of separation anxiety arrives when a baby is between seven and nine months. Frequently, however, there is an earlier episode when a baby is three to four months old. It is just at this age when your baby is beginning to know you are more important than anyone or anything in the world. As this concept of special mother-ness gels for him, he becomes increasingly aware of the different-ness of others.

At this stage, a baby's definition of different-ness can become all inclusive. Anyone who is not *you* qualifies as "stranger": a friendly neighbor, a regular baby-sitter, a beloved grandmother. He will accept no substitutes. His dawning sense of "mother" may even temporarily eclipse a father's role.

"It's hard for me to be away from Lucy at all these days," says Elizabeth. "She needs *me*. I'm the only one who can comfort her when she's upset. It makes Jonathan feel pretty useless. He says, 'O.K. She's in a Mommy-stage.' But I can see it hurts him."

If you have never seen a baby experiencing stranger anxiety, it can be truly upsetting to witness this in your own baby. As his timidity escalates into fear, alarm, and panic, you will wonder what happened to him. Has he been hurt? Bitten? Stung? Is he sick? Has someone frightened him when you weren't there? In an attempt to protect your baby, you may decide to limit his contact with the outside world.

"Going to the market has become an ordeal," says Maggie. "Jack is a magnet for strangers, and when they come up close to him, he screams bloody murder. I want to make a sign that says DON'T TOUCH!"

"When Emma screeched at her grandfather he was so embarrassed. And hurt," says Nan. "He tried to make light of it and said, 'Oh, a Mama's girl.' But it was so uncomfortable. I didn't know what to say."

To be rejected by a baby's screams of protest and fear is awkward for anyone and most adults will be embarrassed. It may appear as if that affectionate fan has done something awful. Or that the baby doesn't like him. Some people take it personally. Many become defensive and even critical of the baby's dependence on his mother. It's not easy to have your baby reject someone. Especially if that person is close to you. As the gracious, adored movie star, your baby made you proud. But as the strident protestor, he may make you feel uneasy and uncomfortable yourself.

When your baby is fearful, he needs your sensitive, understanding support more than ever. Instead of encouraging him to be sociable with others, focus on him yourself. Hold him close to you and quietly tell him it's alright. He needs your physical touch and your reassurance. Though his fear of "strangers" and of separation may be exaggerated and illogical, it is real to him.

Even adults have irrational fears, and new parents in particular. They may fear losing their spouses or their babies or both. They describe terrible dreams of forgetting, misplacing, or abandoning their babies. Many report having random, morbid thoughts of calamity or abduction. These exaggerated and illogical adult fears may reflect an illogical world, but they also speak to the intense attachment a parent feels for his or her child and family.

An adult can talk about his fears, understand and manage them. But a baby can do little with his fears except cry and cling. So, respect your baby's fears and treat him with tender reassurance. Let him cling. Take him gently away from whomever he perceives as the offender. Hold him, rock him, sing to him, calm him. If he's in his stroller, bend down or kneel by his side, close to his eye level. Talk to him in gentle, even tones. Tell him that you are there, that he is safe, and that the world is friendly. Don't whisk him away and "save" him. Intense reactions like these may reinforce or even refuel his distress. Calmly take him back from "the other's" arms for an extra dose of you until he feels secure again. He will slowly feel more confident and social, but he may need to remain close to you for some time.

"When Jack and I go to visit my family," says Maggie, "the door opens and it's—WHOOSH!—everyone rushes him. They push in to see who can get closer. Each one talks louder than the next to see who can get a reaction. They are all smiling and making faces and poking him. It's no wonder he starts to cry."

It can help everyone involved if you pave the way for your baby with some advance preparation. Tell your family or visitors that your baby needs extra time and space to warm up. That he *is* in a "Mommy-stage." This can encourage people to respect your baby's feelings and participate on his level.

No matter when it hits, stranger and separation anxiety in its heightened form can last one to two months or more. During this time it can be trying to have your baby continually clinging to your neck, needing you like a life jacket, but it's important to remain your baby's ally. Don't try to convince him there's nothing to be afraid of or try to prove that he'll be alright in someone else's arms.

"Eric is six months," says Leslie. "He's never had a problem with anyone. What does it mean if he doesn't have stranger anxiety? Does it mean he's not attached enough to me?"

The quality of a baby's attachment to his mother cannot be gauged by the existence or intensity of his separation protest. His attachment does not depend simply on whether you are with him full-time or work outside of the home. Stranger anxiety does not depend on whether your baby has had a full and active social life or has led a quiet, protected existence to date. Nor is stranger anxiety a measure of how well- or maladjusted a baby is. Recent evidence has shown that some babies are temperamentally shy, predisposed to separation anxiety. And there are those babies whose personalities predispose them to respond to separation in a mild way. Aware of the other-ness of "strangers," these babies somehow ride out any misgivings they may have. Some babies respond with fatigue, retreating into grogginess or sleep. And some will show a more active interest and curiosity in novelty, exhibiting little anxiety throughout the first year. Regardless of how it manifests itself, your baby's separation reaction is not something you can control or even avoid. But you can help your baby to get through it. Remember that it is a normal, and passing, stage of growing up.

❧ CLASSIC SEPARATION ANXIETY

While a smaller percentage of babies exhibit stranger anxiety during their third or fourth month, most babies will experience some separation anxiety during their seventh, eighth, or ninth month. It is no coincidence that this is when babies are beginning to crawl. For the first time a baby can explore at will. While he may have free range of only a kitchen or living room, it is an exciting, and at times frightening, big world. A baby may be able to crawl away from his mother, but he is not always sure what distance feels safe and tolerable.

As he explores the world, you are the star by which your baby navigates. He will determine your exact location before taking a turn here, a crawling step there. Your baby may crawl away, look around, and then scurry back to touch your knee or give you a toy or piece of lint, a symbolic connector, and go off again. Sometimes a baby will crawl confidently across the room and then suddenly freeze and dissolve into tears. It is as if he has crossed an emotional boundary line into uncharted waters. He feels stranded, at sea, unmoored. He needs his mother to rescue him.

Mothers may feel frustrated and trapped during this phase. They cannot shift their focus to the mail or a telephone call without hearing about it. They cannot hand off the baby to a trusted other with ease as was possible before. They cannot leave the house without heart-wrenching scenes. They cannot even go to the bathroom without wails of protest.

"I never expected it, but Justin's having some stranger anxiety with my mother," says Jane. "The other day when she arrived, Justin started to cry. Mom went to comfort him but he cried until I took him in my arms. My mother and I were both surprised. Justin's always been so comfortable with her, so connected. I think Mom was a little miffed. I was trying to make her feel better *and* trying not to show how pleased I felt that Justin wanted me."

Separation anxiety requires two people. Both parent and child participate as they each step around the amount of closeness and separateness that feels right. When a baby clings to his mother and won't go to anybody else, some mothers, like Jane, feel favored and confirmed, secretly thinking, "That's my boy." Others look for the trapdoor and think, "Whoa! I can't be at my baby's beck and call like this. I want him to be more independent." Most mothers experience some degree of both of these opposing reactions.

"Recently Sarah has been happy to be by herself in her crib for an hour in the mornings," says Marta. "I hear her cooing and gabbing away. At first I loved that she's so content by herself but then I began to worry that she's not calling out for me, that she doesn't need me. I wonder if it has to do with losing her birth mother."

Adoptive parents struggle with whether to attribute clinginess or aloofness to the early separation their child has had. Adopted children will be sensitive to issues regarding separation and attachment their whole lives. But in this case, confident on her own, Sarah seems to be adapting well. Many babies practice and play with sounds when they first wake up in the morning. Alone and alert, they will babble and gurgle contently for long stretches. Some mothers count their blessings that their babies are content for some time on their own at an early age. Because of her work schedule, however, Marta has limited time with Sarah and misses their treasured morning hour together. In the balance of this equation, time for mother and baby together comes first and we encourage Marta to go to her daughter when she hears that she is awake.

∽ SAYING GOOD-BYE

During the months when your baby is particularly sensitive to your leave-takings, allow extra time for slower transitions. Ask your baby-sitter to arrive thirty minutes earlier than usual and to spend that time with you and the baby. Tell your baby that you will be leaving and, when the time comes, involve him in the good-byes.

If your baby is happily involved with his baby-sitter, you may think it is in his best interests to sneak out the door unnoticed. But this is a short-term solution. When your baby realizes that you are gone, he may become unable to relax, he may become distracted and unable to connect with the baby-sitter or fully engage in play. He may feel that he must be on the lookout for you. He may feel that unless he is vigilant, you disappear. By involving your baby in the process of saying good-bye, by taking extra time with saying good-bye, you communicate that you can tolerate the unease of separation and that he can too. This, in itself, can be a reassuring message to a child. Your baby's repeated experiences with your leave-takings builds his sense of trust that you will not suddenly disappear and that you will always come home.

Use language to prepare your baby about your comings and goings. Say good-bye with confidence. Reassure your baby that you will be back and that all is well. The first few times, waving "bye-bye" may not seem to help. Your baby may give you a quizzical look, then wail and strain to get out of the sitter's arms. But eventually this ritual will serve its purpose. Waving good-bye becomes something your baby can do to participate in what would otherwise be the passive experience of being left. He has played a part in your leaving. After you are gone, he may need some extra holding, and it's important that the sitter provide this. What you do not see after you have shut the door is that, after a good-bye routine, your baby will eventually shift his attention to his caregiver and is then free to reengage in play.

∽ AND GOODNIGHT

Your child may experience nighttime as a difficult separation. And most sleep disturbances for babies six to twelve months have some element of separation anxiety to them. Allow for some extra holding and extra time together at bedtime. Separation anxiety need not change your goals for your baby's sleeping patterns but you need to be sensitive to his heightened vulnerabilities during this stage. You might begin the bedtime routine a little earlier so that it can last a little longer. Many mothers say they check in more frequently than they normally would. Also, make sure your baby's favorite blanket or stuffed animal is close at hand. If he does not have a treasured other, you can actively encourage him to adopt one. Choose something soft and cuddly. Hold it close to him during nursing or bottle feeding. Put it in the crib with your baby. Say goodnight to it too. You can't force this attachment, but many babies quickly respond to this kind of encouragement.

During separation anxiety it can be easier for a baby to let go of his father than his mother. If your baby is engaged in a nightly separation struggle with you, it can be a good time for the father to be more involved at bedtime. We often advise fathers to take over the bedtime routine and check-ins. While a baby loves his father, he may be less ambivalent about letting go. This can be a relief to both mother and baby.

⟨ω SEPARATED ATTACHMENT

"I find myself both craving and fearing time alone, just for me," says Maggie. "I'm desperate for a break, but I can't make myself take one. Occasionally I'll tell Tom, 'I just need to get out for a walk by myself.' He'll say, 'Go!' So I do. At first it feels great. I feel free. But if I don't have an errand to accomplish or a distraction, I walk around feeling aimless and scattered, not myself, not whole. I used to love my time by myself just to wander and browse, but I don't know how to be alone anymore."

It makes sense that as a new mother you may not be able to enjoy formerly treasured pastimes and that, when out on your own, your mind circles back to your baby. You may not feel the exhilaration you anticipated at your freedom. Unencumbered, you may feel naked. But, as you go out more regularly, you will become accustomed to that strange and strained feeling of separated attachment.

"I leave and I can't wait to get home," says Alicia. "It's like when I finally get him to sleep. At first I say, 'Ahhh' and then I feel sad. I miss him. I can't wait for him to wake up. When I do go out I know he's in good hands. But that doesn't seem to make a difference."

"I've started going to the gym twice a week," says Leslie. "I was worried about leaving Eric. But I also wanted him to get used to it. It was hard at first, but if he has his blanket and his pacifier, he does fine. And if I have a specific plan, like exercise, it's great to have a little time to myself."

Leslie's example illustrates how important it is for a mother to take time away from her baby to refuel and care for herself. Ultimately this time apart can help a mother be more available to her baby. There are examples, however, of parents who spend too much time separated from their babies.

∽ TOO MUCH SEPARATION

The question of how much time apart from your baby is possible without sacrificing that crucial attachment and important closeness is a difficult one. Contemporary life for many families demands that both parents pursue their jobs full-time and thus are faced with this question daily. In our work at the Soho Parenting Center we have known many families that fit this profile and we have heard about a variety of parental juggling acts. We have known parents who have worked hard to ensure time with their babies despite the demands of their careers. They have created new balances, they have new priorities and have made significant shifts in their work and social lifestyle in order to be with their babies. Many husband-wife teams have shared in the daily care of their babies in unprecedented ways. We have also known parents swept up in the quest of the modern myth to "have it all," who do not seem able to carve out time to be with their babies. Dedicated to their professions or consumed with their jobs, these parents leave home early, come home late, travel for work, spend weekends exhausted or otherwise engaged, and depend on child care to hold the pieces together at home. Babies can tolerate this kind of absence temporarily and can even thrive with other sensitive caregivers, but over time a baby's primary attachment to his parents will suffer from too much separation. During the first years especially, a child's needs for time with his parents are significant. It is important that parents not underestimate their primary role in the lives of their babies and children and that they recognize the impact of their decisions about time spent with and away from their children.

∽ TRANSITIONAL OBJECTS

Just at the stage when a baby may find it achingly difficult to separate from his mother, he acquires the ability to

adopt something to help him. Typically he chooses something soft, cuddly, or satiny, like a stuffed animal or baby
blanket. Most commonly he prefers it unwashed, potent
with the smells of having been slept with, sucked on, and
held tight. Whatever the chosen object—be it a blanket, a
stuffed animal, a pillow, or a little piece of material—it becomes animated with life and love. The child becomes so
attached to it that everyone in his world knows it by name,
and asks after Blankie, Snuggly, Amma, Tink, Nigh-Nigh,
Noing-Noing, Raggy, Binky, or Tee-Tee. Over half of all
boys and girls adopt a transitional object sometime in their
first two years. About half of these do so before they are
one. Many babies soothe themselves at an earlier age by
sucking their thumb or a pacifier. But at this later age, self-
soothing takes on a different, more intense, meaning.

If your child has adopted a transitional object, he will
develop a ritualized pattern of self-comforting with it.
This usually includes some form of sucking or movement,
something soft to hold or stroke, something which mimics
being soothed by you. In this way, he associates his special object with the way you feed him, rock him, and
hold him close to you. He imbues his treasured other with
nothing less than "mother-ness," and her magical powers
to soothe. It becomes his comfort fetish. Even as a confident preschooler, his transitional object allows him to be
comforted like a baby, soothed and patted as he was once.

A Blanket, a Seal, a Bear, and a Bunny

Parents have been known to turn their houses upside
down looking for a misplaced Miney; to retrace miles
looking for a lost Raggy or Tinks; to keep doubles of treasured Ammas. Baby-sitters are introduced to Di-Dis and

instructed about their revered place in the child's heart. A baby shows his passionate devotion to his blanket every day. He will throw himself onto it, wrap himself up in it, suck it, hug it, and sleep with it. As a baby becomes a toddler and a preschooler, the relationship continues. Even shredded and threadbare, the beloved object retains its power to soothe and comfort. Parents know the importance and power of their child's transitional object but to best describe the passionate devotion a child feels for his beloved other, as well as the various transitional roles it can serve, we interviewed some young children.

A four-year-old girl who is enamored of her blanket described what it means to her in this way. "I love Tee-Tee because it's tickly," she says, pointing to the delicate fringe which she trails across her cheek. "I can use it to tickle me instead of my mother tickling me. Tee-Tee was new when I was a baby. She has the same birthday as me."

A five-year-old boy recalls the loss of his beloved stuffed animal seal. "Once we lost Sealy and I cried so much. My dad walked back all of our steps but he couldn't find him. At naptime I didn't want to sleep with anything else, so I couldn't go to sleep. At the end of the day my dad came home holding a big bag. It was a seal that looked exactly like Sealy but it was newer. I am still sad about losing the old Sealy, but I love this one as much as the other one."

A seven-year-old girl describes her feelings about the formerly pink, now gray, teddy bear she proudly displays. "I love Teddy. I love him as much as I love my mom and my dad and my sister. I got him when I was born. I know that he is not alive, but I feel like he is. I still talk to him. If I drop him, I say I'm sorry. I don't do that with my other stuffed animals. It is strange. Sometimes when I get hurt, my little sister runs and gets Teddy for me. Teddy makes me feel better. He's always there for me when I'm upset. It's like having a second mom or dad."

Many adults fondly remember their treasured stuffed animals and blankets. Some still have them. A woman in her late twenties describes the enduring power of her long-ago feelings for a beloved, stuffed animal rabbit.

"The thing I remember best about Bunny was its color. It was a peachy pink and the ears were lined with satin. Really soft satin. I would hold those ears up next to my face, suck my thumb, and go into La-La land. Eventually the satin wore off but I still loved it. As I got older I remember becoming aware that I had to stop sucking my thumb and I had to separate from Bunny. I remember Bunny becoming less magical, less alive. It's like when you begin to know there is no Santa Claus. The feelings were still all there but it wasn't the same. I could never put that rabbit away, though. I even took it with me to college. I think my mother got a kick out of that."

Tee-Tee, Sealy, Teddy, and Bunny are testaments to a child's imagination, passion, and drive toward independence. With mother held close in their hearts and minds, a blanket or bear held close in their arms, all is well with the world.

This is our last session, the end of this group as we have known it. In the process of concluding, each woman takes a last turn at reflecting on issues of attachment and separation and how they affect her.

"I think *I* need a transitional object," Maggie says.

The women laugh but Maggie insists, "No, really. I need something to hold on to because I can't seem to put

Jack down. People comment all the time that he seems attached to me. And they mean *physically* attached. The thing is I worry that something bad will happen to him if I'm not holding him. I know this is my weak spot now and that I'm putting my own fears onto Jack, but I have to constantly fight that in myself."

Periodic feelings of heightened responsibility are not uncommon for new parents. Newly aware of the preciousness of life, they are also acutely conscious of its precariousness. You may find yourself checking to see if your baby is breathing while he sleeps. Or double- and triple-checking his car seat. But if you cannot let him out of your sight or arms for a moment, and never feel comfortable otherwise, something other than responsibility is lurking in the wings of your imagination. If you have worries that seem unreasonable to your logical mind but that carry weight emotionally, if you feel compelled to act on your emotions rather than choose to, read this as a flag marking your hot spots, or as Maggie terms them, your "weak spots."

"My weak spot is that I'm too bonded with Emma," says Nan. "Rick tells me that all the time. In some ways he's right. But it's hard to draw the line between what is the right amount of love and what is too much. When Rick accuses me of being too intense with Emma, I get defensive. He'll never have the same preoccupation with her that I do, so how can he understand? I know for me it has to do with my mother's death. Sometimes I can't look at Emma without thinking about my mother. It's easier for me to talk about all of this in here than with Rick. I don't feel as defensive. But I know letting go is going to be one of those things I have to work on all the time now that I am a mother."

"When I was a kid I *only* got unqualified, loving attention when I was sick or very sad," says Marta. "I think some of my happiest times were when I was home from school on a sick day. I remember my mother indulging me and it felt wonderful. What could be wrong with totally loving your child? My instinct as a mother is to give Sarah all my attention and love all the time that I have her."

"I guess what makes the difference is how the mother feels about all of this separation stuff," Leslie comments. "I've been considering going out of town to a workshop for two days and one night. My mother says, 'How can you leave your husband and baby?' It makes *her* more uncomfortable than it does me. I've always been able to leave easily. None of my brothers or sisters wanted to go away to college. But I did. And I was the only one that left my hometown. When I go away from my husband or from the baby I always want to come back, and I wouldn't want to stay away for very long. But I think being apart can be a good thing."

"Time is going by so quickly," says Ronnie. "I know I should really be focusing on how great it is that Elyse is growing up. But the truth is I want her to stay little forever. In the hospital Elyse slept with me in my arms. That was the most wonderful feeling in the world. I'll never forget it. And nursing. Well, you know how I feel about nursing. These are the things I don't want to end."

"I don't want this group to end," Jessica blurts out. "I've become so attached to it. It's been great for me. Now that Nell's colic is over I know I can manage on my own, but I think I'd be having separation anxiety if we weren't going to be getting together again. I hate good-byes."

"I remember when my sister's child learned to wave

good-bye," Alicia says. "I was baby-sitting for her. My sister and her husband went out and I was holding their baby and we were waving good-bye. The baby was waving her little hand and it was so cute and then my sister burst into tears. It seemed ridiculous to me at the time. I didn't get it. Now I get it."

Alicia pauses for a moment, then resumes. "I just flashed on the good-bye scenes we used to have when my parents left on their European travels. We weren't allowed to be sad. Mother and Father gave us these little lectures about self-reliance and being grown up. I remember biting my tongue so I wouldn't cry. I like the feeling of strength and independence that I got from them, but I want to be more there for Keith, more sensitive to how he is feeling."

"I wanted to tell you that Christmas ended up going much better than I had expected," says Elizabeth. "I had been so wound up about it, remember? I didn't want to repeat the scene I had last time we visited my parents in D.C. But I also couldn't imagine Christmas without them. So Jonathan and I had everyone to our place for Christmas. And it was much better on our turf. Everyone was well behaved and I felt more like an adult than a child. It was the best of all worlds: my husband, my baby, my sister, and my parents, all in *my* house."

"Yeah," says Jane. "I've always felt safest in my own house. I was eleven the first time I spent the night at a friend's. She lived in the same apartment building as I did, and from her window I could see across the courtyard into my apartment. I remember staring into my windows and crying. I've always thought of myself as such a Mama's girl. I had to have my mother stay with me until I fell asleep every night. I think I cried every morning before kindergarten. But now I'm realizing it probably had as much to do with my mother not wanting me to leave her as it did with me not wanting to leave my mother.

"My parents didn't have the most wonderful relationship in the world," Jane continues. "So I became everything to my mother. And she gave her all to me too. She was the Girl Scout leader and the school crossing guard and the class mother. But I guess she just couldn't let go. Even when I tried to be more independent I always had this tugging feeling, pulling me back to her. I don't want Justin to be like I was. I want him to have lots of friends. To feel secure. To have adventures. Even though it may sound to you like my mother is as much in my life as ever, it feels more balanced now that I have Justin. I still need my mother and she still needs me, but I have my own life now."

⟶ FULL CIRCLE

The act of birth is a form of separation. A mother pushes her baby out, expels him. The cord is cut. For nine months, mother and child have lived together and now they are separate beings. But the act of birth is perhaps easier than truly letting go of your own child. As with attachment, separation is a process that can last a lifetime. It is neither linear nor logical, but moves forward and backward, marked with regressions and phases of physical neediness, with bursts of self-confidence and venturings out.

One of the biggest challenges of parenting during the second half of the first year is the need to shift between giving to your baby when he is clinging to you and letting him move away from you when he is learning to crawl and walk. Sometimes you will feel much more comfortable with his need to be with you and less tolerant of his desire to be out in the world. Other times you will love your baby's independence and feel provoked by his neediness.

The processes of attachment and separation are not distinct and independent lines of development, but are jumbled up together, a welter of emotions. Each is mixed up with the joys and fears of the other. But for each tie you let loose, a new one is formed. A new way of loving, communicating, and connecting.

"One day when my niece was about eleven months old, she clung to her mother's legs all morning long chanting, 'Mama, Mama,' " says Alicia. "She must have said it a hundred times. Then, she took her first steps. And within days she was walking. It was amazing to see."

A baby's growth during his first year is fast and furious. Attachment spawns separation, and his motivation for independence is matched perhaps only by his drive for love. After weeks and weeks of practicing his walking, with your back curved over his tiny shoulders, gripping tightly to your fingers, he will one day unclasp his hold and take his first toddling steps. Throughout his growing up he will have spurts and rushes of development like these as well as tender moments of needy regression.

A mother's growth during her first year of motherhood is also fast and furious. Everything has changed for her. And she must change too. As your baby takes his first steps, you may clap and smile and reward him with kisses while a part of you is saddened at the thought of him walking away from you. As your baby waves his hand bye-bye to you, you may want to cry too. But a part of you will always go with him as he goes out into the world.

Life comes full circle as you take on the mantle of parenthood, as you see yourself in your baby's shining eyes, as your own parents become graying grandparents, as you dedicate yourself to your new family. Each day of parenthood you leave your childhood behind and embrace it again in a new way. Your new attachments, responsibilities, and confidences carve your life, shape it and build it. Your baby is a new era, a new possibility, a new you.